An African Centered Response to Ruby Payne's Poverty Theory

by Dr. Jawanza Kunjufu

Chicago, Illinois

Introduction   vi i

1. Ruby Payne's Position   1

2. White Poverty   21

3. Black Poverty   29

4. Economic Empowerment   47

5. School Funding   73

6. Integration   89

7. Educational Solutions   103

References   159

Index   165

DEDICATION

This book is dedicated to the following:

African American children who were not blessed to be born in economic affluence or parented by both a mother and a father.

African American mothers who do not possess a college degree and are unable to stay at home to raise their children.

African American schools that receive less than $15,000 per student and whose teachers lack a master's degree or better in the subjects they've been assigned to teach.

Families that have been forced to file lawsuits against state governments that still use property taxes to fund schools. States are supposed to be the great equalizer in providing a quality education for all children, but many still rely on property taxes to fund schools and educate children. This is illegal, unfortunate, and criminal.

Jonathan Kozol, author of several excellent books, including *Savage Inequality* and *Shame of a Nation.* He understands, unlike Ruby Payne, that the problem is not low-income families but poorly funded schools.

Education Trust, a research organization that has done excellent work documenting the importance of teacher quality.

Rev. James Meeks, Illinois state senator, executive vice president of Operation PUSH, and pastor of Salem Baptist Church in Chicago, one of the largest churches in America. Rev. Meeks strongly disagrees with how the state of Illinois funds education. It is one thing for authors like myself and Jonathan Kozol and research organizations like the Education Trust to write about the inequities. It is another for activists to take the struggle to the street. Rev. Meeks promised Governor Rod Blagojevich that if he didn't do something to ensure more equitable financing of schools in the state of Illinois, he would run for the governor's seat. This was no idle threat. Because Governor Blagojevich knew he could not win without the Black vote, he acquiesced and promised to identify new strategies, including using funds from the tollway system, to provide a more equitable allocation of money to low-income schools.

Rev. Jesse Jackson, president of Operation PUSH. Rev. Jackson identified at least one school in Chicago with crumbling facilities. In the same school district, a magnet school enjoyed state-of-the-art facilities, including a functional swimming pool, science labs, musical instruments, qualified, competent, and experienced teachers, an abundance of current textbooks, and an excellent gymnasium. Rev. Jackson brought media attention to one school in particular where there was no water in the swimming pool. It was being used as a storage area. The gymnasium was so poorly lit that you couldn't see whether the ball went into the basket or not. The science labs were nonfunctional. There were no musical instruments. There weren't enough textbooks to go around, and many teachers were not qualified to teach the subjects they had been assigned.

In the spirit of Frederick Douglass, power concedes nothing without a struggle. Rev. Jackson and Operation PUSH put pressure on the superintendent of schools. Before the school year concluded, Jesse Jackson was swimming in the pool, an adequate supply of current textbooks and musical instruments had been secured, the gymnasium was lit, and the administration promised that the lab would be functional and teachers would be qualified.

I pray this book gives activists such as Rev. Meeks and Rev. Jackson more ammunition. There is a need for research, but there is also a need for activism.

INTRODUCTION

I am an educational consultant to numerous school districts nationwide. Schools bring me in to help them design and implement strategies to close the achievement gap between White and African American students. I also provide workshops on reducing the number of African American males in special education and suspension and on the dropout rolls. Schools have hundreds of consultants to choose from. I have been blessed with being in high demand for more than 30 years.

Over the past several years, I have noticed that some schools have been bringing in Ruby Payne, an educational consultant who believes that poverty is the major factor affecting the outcome of children's academic achievements. Let me say here and now that I have nothing personal against Ruby Payne. In fact, I agree with some of her theories, and I acknowledge her contribution to the goal of closing the academic achievement gap.

Ruby Payne grew up in middle-class Mennonite communities in Indiana and Ohio. She was a high school English teacher and married a bond trader. She later became a school principal in an affluent school district in Illinois, and it was this experience that shaped her thinking on the impact of poverty and wealth on academic performance. She then moved to Texas and became the director of professional development for a school district near Houston.

In 1995 she wrote her best seller, *A Framework for Understanding Poverty*. It received an excellent response, and she went on to write several other books. She now employs 25 trainers and provides additional work for 50 consultants nationwide.

More than 30 years ago, my late mentor, Dr. Barbara Sizemore, gave me the following paradigm to use in my work with schools:

1. Problem
2. Cause
3. Solution
4. Implementation

I first ask clients to describe the problem they want me to address. They usually mention the academic gap between their African American and White students: the 200-point difference on the SAT and the three-stanine difference on elementary school achievement exams. They also will mention that African American males are only 8 percent of the student population nationwide but represent 33 percent of students placed in special education, suspended, and expelled. Even worse, 40 to 60 percent of African American males are dropping out of school altogether.

Dr. Sizemore taught me to have schools diagnose causes before offering solutions. This process weeds out the politically correct discussions and reveals what administrators and teachers truly think about students, their families, and the community at large. It makes no sense to design strategies without knowing first what teachers' and administrators' preconceived notions about African American students are. For example, if teachers believe low-income is the major cause for the achievement gap, it would be futile to provide a workshop on raising expectations. If they believe the lack of a father in the home or the educational background of the mother is the cause of low academic performance, it would be counterproductive to recommend increasing time on task. I first have to address the

Introduction

preconceived ideas about African American children, families, and communities before moving forward.

In Dr. Sizemore's paradigm, solutions must always address the causes. This may seem obvious, but all too often schools will diagnose a problem correctly but then lack the will to implement strong, relevant solutions.

Some educators agree with Ruby Payne that poverty is the cause of the academic achievement gap. Others believe that mothers not possessing a college degree contribute to low academic performance. In analyzing why a student is not performing at potential or why a school ranks at the low end of standardized tests, these assessments may be correct. Or they may not. Often snap judgments are made based on an educator's or administrator's personal experience and value system, creating a limited lens with which to view the issues. Thus this step in the process, finding out what teachers and administrators believe, is absolutely necessary in helping me get to the root of the problem.

Public schools that serve low-income communities are not all the same; however, I find the same problems over and over again in schools that are failing African American students. The usual culprits are as follows: poor school leadership, low teacher expectations, low student time on task, irrelevant curriculums, an abundance of left-brain lesson plans, an individualistic vs. communal student approach, and coed classrooms.

To these schools, I offer the following relevant strategies: strong school leadership, high teacher expectations, increased student time on task, a more relevant Africentric, multicultural curriculum, more right-brain lesson plans, utilization of cooperative learning, and single-gender classrooms. In the spirit of Dr. Sizemore's paradigm, the solutions always address the causes.

Clearly, Ruby Payne and I understand the academic achievement gap differently. Ruby Payne blames poverty; I see many dimensions to the problem, including the larger social issues of racism and capitalism. I come from an African-centered perspective while her perspective is Eurocentric. She admits her poverty theory was shaped by her own experiences as a teacher and administrator. My framework has evolved out of a sizable body of research that documents what works with African American children—as well as my experience as an educator and consultant for schools and school districts.

How convenient to choose poverty, the number of parents in the home, or the educational background of the mother as major reasons for the academic achievement gap. Ironically, teachers and administrators have no control over these factors.

Deficit Model
I don't want to focus on poverty. I want to study what some schools do in low-income areas to produce children who succeed on tests well above the national average. I fully understand why some schools would rather focus on poverty than how raising expectations, increasing time on task, infusing the curriculum with Africentricity, increasing right-brain lesson plans, and implementing single-gender classrooms would narrow the academic achievement gap between African American and White students. Blaming poverty requires little work. You don't have to adjust your lesson plans or raise expectations. It's much easier to have a good time blaming the victim, and in America, that has an historical precedent.

In 1971, William Ryan wrote the book *Blaming the Victim.* Ryan observed,

Introduction

In education, we have programs of compensatory education to build up the skills and attitudes of the ghetto child rather than structural changes in the schools. In race relations we have social engineers to think up ways to strengthen the Negro family rather than methods of eradicating racism.[1]

Ryan's theory is especially valuable in exposing the ideological base of *deficit thinking*, where the powerful blame the innocent. He shows us how deficit thinking translates to action.

1. Social problems were identified (by victim blamers).
2. A study was done in order to find out how the disadvantaged and advantaged were different.
3. Once the differences were identified, they were defined as the causes of the social problem.
4. Governmental intervention was put in play to correct the differences.

The great appeal of deficit thinking as a model of social reform in the 1960s and early 1970s lay in the framework's appearance of soundness. All of this occurred so smoothly that it seemed downright rational.

As deficit theorists began searching for more cultural explanations for failure in school and life, many turned to the work of anthropologist Oscar Lewis and his "culture of poverty" theory. Lewis wrote a series of studies on the urban poor in Mexico, New York, Puerto Rico, and Cuba. He emphasized that people living in poverty tend to create a unique self-sustaining lifestyle or way of life marked by a host of negative values, norms, and social practices. The culture of poverty that is allegedly passed on to successive generations consisted of 70 traits, which can be compressed into four clusters:

1. Basic attitudes, values, and character structure of poor people.
2. The nature of the poor's family system.
3. The nature of the slum community.
4. The poor's civil and social relationship with the larger society.[2]

Lewis' list of the cultural traits of the poor evokes a powerful, negative image of them as lazy, fatalistic, hedonistic, violent, distrustful people living in common law unions and in dysfunctional, female-centered, authoritarian families. The poor are chronically unemployed and rarely participate in local civic activities, vote, or trust the police and political leaders.

Lewis argued that the poor created an autonomous, distinct subculture or way of life that had become encapsulated and self-perpetuating over generations. Ultimately, the poor's way of life, which is allegedly inferior to the mainstream way of life, kept them impoverished. For anyone wanting to indict the poor, the culture of poverty theory is a powerful metaphor that spawns a sweeping, holistic image. It provides policy makers and the general public with a relatively non-technical yet scientific way to categorize and characterize all poor people.

Ruby Payne's theory is nothing but a warmed up version of Ryan's idea of blaming the victim and Oscar Lewis' research on poverty. Those who want to study poverty may go to Ryan and Lewis, where they can study the 70 to 100 traits.

This book is an African-centered response to poverty theories and deficit thinking, and I make no apologies for that. I don't want to study poverty. As Robert Woodson, Sr., wrote

Introduction

in *The Triumphs of Joseph,* we now have "poverty pimps." They can talk about poverty, make money off of poverty, and write books on poverty. They can do everything but solve poverty. Throughout this book we will instead study economic empowerment. If people are so concerned about poverty, then we should teach poor people how to acquire wealth in America. We should explain to poor people how it came to be that 1 percent of the population owns 57 percent of the wealth and 10 percent owns 86 percent of the wealth. The remaining 90 percent only owns 14 percent of the wealth.

It is obvious that some people would rather talk, study, and have workshops on poverty than solve the problem. It's understandable. Eradicating poverty would mean eliminating their positions.

Defining Africentricity

Let me define what I mean by African-centered. My good friend and eminent professor at Temple University, Molefi Asante, is the father of the concept of Afrocentricity. When you are African-centered, you no longer see the world through another person's eyes. You see the world through your own perspective. Let me give you some examples of what it means to understand history and the world from an African-centered perspective.

America teaches that Columbus came here in 1492. The African-centered perspective would want to know when Africans first arrived in the "New World." You must understand that this world may have been new to Europeans but was fairly well-known to Africans and others. Read the work of Ivan Van Sertima, *They Came Before Columbus,* to learn about the Olmec civilization. Africans had traveled to America as early as 800 B.C.

When you're African-centered, you empathize with six million Jews dying in the Holocaust, but you also want to know how many Africans died in America during our holocaust, the *Maafa*. Historians believe the figure may be as low as 10 million or as high as 100 million. Most African historians agree that around 30 million Africans died in the slave trade.

Where is Upper Egypt? In the north or the south of the country? That would depend on your frame of reference. If you're African-centered and you understand that the Nile River flows from the south to the north, Upper Egypt is in the south, not the north.

America teaches the lie that Hippocrates, who was born around 500 B.C., was the first doctor. African scholarship says that Imhotep, born 2800 B.C., was the first doctor.

Schools glorify Pythagoras, who was born 600 B.C., as the father of mathematics. African scholarship teaches that the true father of mathematics was Ahmose, who was born 1600 B.C.

Thus, this book is an African-centered response to Ruby Payne's poverty theory.

Talking about poverty does not help African American children. From an African-centered perspective, I see only two courses. We look at what successful schools have done in low-income areas to produce African American children that perform above the national average, and we economically empower African American children and their families to rise out of the mire and squalor of poverty.

I've written more than 26 books on a myriad of subjects, including education and economics. When I first began writing and offering workshops, the purpose was to arm educators with strategies they could use to help African American children. I didn't know that I would also have to develop a

Introduction

framework and strategies for understanding poverty and economically empowering the Black community.

Ruby Payne's theory does neither. Her theory is based on the idea that there is something wrong with African American children. The deficit model is prescribed and based on the idea that there is something wrong with our children, and we need a workshop to describe what is wrong with them.

When schools bring me in, I quickly inform them that this consultant does not believe that our children are broken or that they have a genetic flaw. The problem is systemic. Isn't it interesting that the achievement gap between Black and White students is smaller in kindergarten than it is in twelfth grade? How does the poverty model reconcile that? How do we explain how poor children enter kindergarten enthusiastic and motivated to learn and yet with each succeeding grade, the questions asked in class decrease, cheating increases, and the desire to drop out becomes more and more of a reality.

Recently, I met with a superintendent who said, "I'm not bringing you in to address our problems K-5. We don't have much of a problem K-5. I'm bringing you in to address our problems 6-12." Did poverty increase for our children in grades 6-12 or was there something wrong with the superintendent's perceptual lens?

It is interesting that in middle-class, affluent, integrated neighborhoods, the racial achievement gap persists. If poverty is the major issue, then how do we explain the racial academic achievement gap in affluent communities such as Ann Arbor (Michigan), Cleveland Heights (Ohio), Shaker Heights (Ohio), Evanston (Illinois), Cambridge (Massachusetts), Montclair (New Jersey), White Plains (New York), Palo Alto (California), and Oak Park (Illinois)?

I'm sure people like Charles Murray, the author of *The Bell Curve,* would say the gap is due to genetics, not poverty. He would probably say that it doesn't matter where African American children live. In his murky lens, they are genetically deficient because they are African American.

The late John Ogbu wrote a powerful book, *Black American Students in an Affluent Suburb.* He was brought in as a consultant and researcher to try and understand the racial academic achievement gap in Shaker Heights, Ohio. Ogbu offered several reasons for the gap, but two among them are the makeup of middle-class families and the influence of peer pressure.

In many White middle-class families, the father works while the mother stays home, raising the children. Father's income is $100,000. Because mother is at home, she's able to monitor homework, visit the school, and hold teachers accountable. She literally becomes her child's assistant teacher.

Many African American families in that same community also make $100,000, but that figure is achieved differently. Father makes $50,000 and mother makes $50,000. They both work 8 to 12 hours per day. Unfortunately, they are not able to spend the same amount of time with their children in coaching homework, monitoring the schools, and being active members of the PTA.

Relationships are everything to our youth, and Ogbu found that peer pressure has a tremendous impact. As I mentioned in my book *To Be Popular or Smart: The Black Peer Group,* many African American youth who are doing well are not encouraged by their peer group. They don't like being the only African American student in AP (advanced placement), honors, or gifted and talented classes. Affluent schools look integrated on the outside—50 percent Black, 50 percent

Introduction

White—but on the inside they are highly segregated due to tracking. White and Asian students dominate AP, honors, and gifted and talented classes. Regular classes are integrated, while Blacks and Hispanics dominate remedial and special education classes.

Many African Americans naively believed that if they simply lived in an affluent community, their educational concerns would be resolved. How does the poverty theory explain the fact that their concerns have not been resolved?

Why do so many of our youth think that being smart is acting White? Could it be because of the Eurocentric curriculum that fails to teach the truth about African history? Children who know their history realize that Africans were the first to contribute to the arts, sciences, technology, and more. Children who know that Imhotep was the first doctor do not associate being smart with acting White.

Does the poverty theory help us to understand why some of our children associate being smart with being White? Or is it much deeper than that? Could it be that even in affluent schools and districts racism, not poverty, still shows its ugly head and teachers lower expectations based on race, not income?

Which schools have the highest placement of African American students in medical schools: Harvard or Howard, Princeton or Prairie View, Yale or Xavier? Based on the poverty theory, the answer should be Harvard, Princeton, and Yale. But the correct answer is Howard, Prairie View, and Xavier. How does the poverty theory account for this?

We will explore Ruby Payne's position in the next chapter, but I would be remiss if I didn't provide an in-depth examination of White poverty. If Ruby Payne is so concerned about poverty, then maybe she should look at the 24 million

Whites who live below the poverty line rather than just the 16 million Blacks and Hispanics.

We will then look at Black poverty and the driving factors behind it. Since it is not enough to study poverty, we will examine some wealth acquisition strategies. Since African American youth live in a capitalistic society, they need to learn the principles of capitalism. They should learn that the tiny percentage of people who own most of the wealth in America did not become rich from an NBA or NFL contract, a rap CD, or selling drugs but from entrepreneurship, real estate, or the stock market.

We will look at the work of Jonathan Kozol. His main areas of concern are how schools are funded and the fact that schools are more segregated today than they were 30 years ago.

We will conclude with numerous strategies on educational empowerment. We will brainstorm ways to implement these strategies and not just sit around the workshop table, drinking coffee and eating doughnuts, describing how poor these children are and how unfortunate it is that they act the way they do.

Let's now look at Ruby Payne's position and dissect it point by point.

CHAPTER 1: RUBY PAYNE'S POSITION

Review the following charts closely because this is the major premise of the poverty theory.

Reading skills on entering kindergarten by race and socioeconomic status

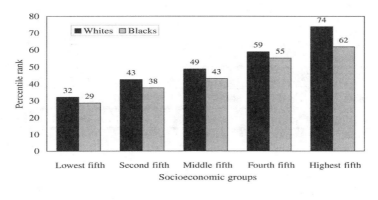

Mathematics skills on entering kindergarten by race and socioeco-nomic status

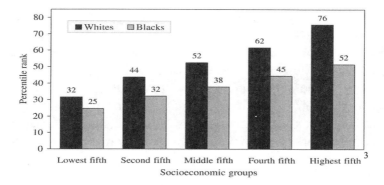

Average SAT Scores

FAMILY INCOME			
Less than $10,000/year	426	458	884
$10,000 - $20,000/year	443	463	906
$30,000 - $40,000/year	480	487	967
$40,000 - $50,000/year	496	500	996
$50,000 - $60,000/year	505	509	1014
$60,000 - $70,000/year	511	515	1026
$70,000 - $80,000/year	517	522	1039
$80,000 - $100,000/year	529	534	1063
More than $100,000/year	554	565	1119 [4]

I am aware that poverty, fatherlessness, and lack of parental education are factors that impact our children's education. In Figure 2b, if we look at the lowest quintile, African American children are only at the 29 percentile in reading. If you look at African American families in the highest quintile, they are as high as 62 percent. It is obvious that income does matter.

If you compare the lowest quintile with each successive quintile based on income, African American achievement increases. It moves from 29 to 38 to 43 to 55 to 62. The chart does not look at any other indicator such as the number of parents in the home, the educational background of the parent(s), the school-per-pupil expenditure, the quality of teachers, their expectations, pedagogy, or curriculum. This chart only looks at one variable, and that's income. Clearly, as income increases, so does academic achievement. The reverse also could be said: as income declines, so does academic achievement.

2

Ruby Payne's Position

I try my best to be an honest researcher, to present all sides of a story. I don't agree with all of Ogbu's findings or all of Jonathan Kozol's arguments on school-per-pupil expenditures and integration. I could have made the decision not to present the above graphs in order to strengthen my position, but that would have been dishonest.

In fact, after researching this issue, I had to ask myself if I really wanted to write a book refuting the poverty theory. Did I really want to remain an educational consultant when teachers have access to charts like these that clearly document the correlations between income and academic achievement?

The answer is yes. I want to remain a consultant. I still believe we can make a difference, regardless of students' income. I would love to work with schools whose African American students live in affluent homes, the fathers are present, and the mothers, who have graduate degrees, stay at home to raise their children.

I am one of the best Bid Whist players in America. I don't play as much as I used to, but I was taught that you have to play the hand you're dealt. The hand that I was dealt has one-third of African American families and half of African American children living below the poverty line. I simply cannot let the poverty theory dictate my approach to improving schools for African American children.

The information in these charts has led Ruby Payne and others to see a correlation between poverty and academic achievement. She has continued the legacy of Ryan and Lewis in trying to help us understand poverty. However, in spite of the reality portrayed by these charts, African American children can succeed and the gap can be narrowed. There are strategies that we can use to empower African American youth.

3

Student-Teacher Relationships

I respect Ruby Payne, and I even agree with some of her ideas. For example, she believes that *the key to achievement for students in poverty is creating relationships with them.* I agree that the relationship between student and teacher is critical. But what if the teacher does not have the child's best interest at heart? What if the teacher is incompetent or not qualified? What if the teacher does not relate well to children?

There are five types of educators in America:

Custodians believe, "I have mine and you have yours to get." Custodians will quickly tell you they have one year, four months, three weeks, and two days left before retirement. They do not have good relationships with students.

Referral agents are quick to refer students to special education. Twenty percent of the teachers make 80 percent of the referrals. Referral agents have poor relationships with students.

Instructors teach subjects, not children. Unfortunately, from the fourth grade on, the number of instructors increases in public schools. This is a systemic problem, and the achievement gap widens, as students get older. Departmentalization also contributes to the problem. Many students do not transition well from elementary school, where they had one teacher for all subjects, to high school, where they have seven different teachers, one for each subject. Instructors should listen to Ruby Payne and establish relationships with their students. Bill Gates' funding of small junior and senior high schools enables powerful relationships between teachers and students to take place. Much more will be said about this in the last chapter on educational solutions.

4

Ruby Payne's Position

Master Teachers understand the importance of subject matter, but they also understand there should be congruence between teaching style and learning style. Giving left brain lesson plans to right-brain-thinking students is a recipe for disaster. More will be said about this in the last chapter.

Coaches understand subject matter and pedagogy, but what makes them so highly effective is that they respect their students, and this enables them to establish strong relationships and maintain high academic expectations. Trust is a key factor in this relationship, and students trust their coaches. Coaches understand and appreciate their student's culture. They visit the home and bond with parents. They motivate their students and encourage them to develop goals.

I agree with Ruby Payne that teachers need to develop a relationship with students. Unfortunately, we have too many custodians, referral agents, and instructors and very few teachers and coaches. Also, custodians, referral agents, and instructors love talking about the deficit model. They believe that the children are broke, financially and spiritually. They refuse to take responsibility for their own shortcomings, preferring instead to place the blame on the children, the parents, the community, etc.

There are many racists among custodians, referral agents, and instructors in public schools today. Workshops and books cannot change attitudes in a day. *You cannot be a multicultural teacher and a one-culture person.* You can't implement Ruby Payne's and Jawanza Kunjufu's theories on culture Monday through Friday from 9:00 am to 3:00 pm and be a racist in the evenings, weekends, and summers. At best, you may be able to pretend that color doesn't matter.

The racist mindset is so prevalent in public schools that I strongly encourage schools and school districts to make diversity training for faculty and staff a priority, and the training must be ongoing. Only the principals that provide strong leadership in this area will see change in their schools; and workshops can provide the catalyst. School leaders must mandate and see to it—on a daily basis—that certain steps are taken. For example, they must visit classrooms and make sure that all students are treated fairly. They must hold teachers accountable. Otherwise, workshops will not change behavior.

Looping Teachers

Ruby Payne and I agree on the practice of *looping teachers.* If children can spend more than one year with a master teacher or coach academic performance will improve. However, looping has a downside. If children are looped with a custodian, referral agent, or instructor for several years, they will suffer. According to many studies, children who come from low-income households, are fatherless, or the mother is illiterate but they are looped with a teacher or coach, perform well above the national average. Children who are looped with a custodian, referral agent, or instructor for several years test below average.

Ruby Payne, the poverty theory does not explain the success we see with the practice of looping teachers. Poverty may not be the most significant variable here. The most significant variable is who the children are looped with.

Culturally Biased Tests

I agree with Ruby Payne that *most tests are culturally biased.* My book *Keeping Black Boys Out of Special Ed* included a full chapter on racial biases in tests. Unfortunately, many schools still use the Wechsler and the Binet, which has been documented, are not in the best interest of children of color. We recommend using SOMPA (System of Multicultural/ Pluralistic Assessment), the CAS (Cognitive Assessment System), the LPAD (Learning Potential Assessment Device), and the Black Intelligence Test.

How would you answer the following questions?

What was Washington's first name? From a Eurocentric perspective, the answer is probably George. From an African-centered perspective, the answer might be Booker T. or Harold.

What color is a banana? From an affluent perspective, a banana is yellow or green. In a poor community, bananas are dark brown.

I agree with you, Ruby Payne. Many tests are culturally biased. Are you advocating that more schools use CAS, SOMPA, LPAD, and the Black Intelligence Test?

Language Register

I agree with Ruby Payne's position on the *language register*. She calls it the "formal register," which in educational terms is defined as Standard English. The "casual register" would be viewed from a Black perspective as Ebonics or Black English.

I agree that our children must be well versed in Standard English. My concern is the approach. I consult with numerous schools in Oakland, California. Several years ago there was a rumor that Oakland schools were trying to teach Black children Ebonics. If you're African-centered, you know this accusation makes no sense. African American children already know Ebonics, so the media reported the story incorrectly.

7

We say our society is multicultural, yet we have a very rigid definition of English. Often I ask teachers what they mean by "Standard" English: that spoken by Prince Charles in England? Ted Kennedy in Boston? Jimmy Carter in Georgia?

Oakland schools were not trying to teach Black children Ebonics since they already knew it. They were trying to teach new, incoming White teachers how to code switch. They were trying to teach them to view African American children as bilingual and intelligent and to allow them to speak what they heard at home. Ebonics is a legitimate dialect, with rules of grammar and syntax, distinctive in its pronunciation and vocabulary, and clearly spoken and understood by a large group of people. This is what White teachers were learning so that they would not respond negatively to students who spoke it. They learned to listen and understand the dialect and then have students translate (orally or in writing) to Standard English.

Some educators believe that the best argument for teaching Black children Standard English is that this is the only way to get a good job downtown from the White man. We will look at this in more detail in the chapter on economic empowerment, but in Hip Hop culture, many Black youth are not totally convinced that education pays. Nor are they convinced that there is a good job downtown from the White man. What they are sure of is that 50 Cent, P Diddy, and Snoop are splitting infinitives all the way to the bank as they earn bling bling.

Let me be clear. If getting a job is your best argument for teaching Standard English, many African Americans will disagree with you. They do not think that speaking Standard English is the best economic strategy.

Classroom Discipline

Ruby Payne says that *many youth in poverty laugh when they are disciplined and like to entertain and become the class clown.* While I slightly agree with her position, let me elaborate on my concern. Many schools bring me in to talk to students, especially male students. They love telling me that the boys have low self-esteem. I beg to differ. There is a distinction between school-esteem and self-esteem.

Many teachers believe in the military's approach to disciplining Black males: break them down then build them back up. But most Black boys won't let you break their spirit. You can send them to the corner or the principal's office, you can suspend or expel them, but they are not going to let anyone break their spirit. Watch males who supposedly have low self-esteem as they maneuver on the playground, the basketball court, in the cafeteria, or anywhere outside of the classroom. You will see them handle a variety of situations with confidence and competence. Isn't this the definition of self-esteem? Boys don't like it when girls are called on more than they are. When girls are asked to collect the papers, pass out pencils, or take a note to the principal's office, boys feel ignored.

Boys may use laughter to protect themselves from dangerous teachers who do not see their value and believe in the deficit model. The same students who love to entertain, who are good at playing the dozens, rapping, and being the class clown really crave attention. Because of the large male ego, boys are either going to be your best or worst students. They want attention. Unfortunately, many have found they will receive more attention by being negative than by being positive. The best strategy to address class clowns is to inform him that you are not going to put him out. Students also act like clowns to cover up their academic deficiency. Challenge him by giving him the last five minutes of class to perform. Most will back down.

Since a class clown loves to be the center of attention, see that as strength and play to it. Put him in a spelling bee or a debate contest. Let him emcee the school assembly or narrate the school play. The list of ways to play to this strength goes on and on. If only we had teachers and coaches who could move children from Black culture to school culture without putting a negative connotation on the former.

Poverty Culture in Schools
Ruby Payne believes that:

One of the reasons it is getting more and more difficult to conduct school as we have in the past is that the students who bring the middle-class culture with them are decreasing in numbers, and the students who bring the poverty culture are increasing in numbers.[5]

This is a strong and prophetic statement. On one hand, it is true that children of all races are less respectful than in past years. We've had an increasing number of children in our schools who do not respect authority. Educators are trained to teach, not to discipline. This becomes even more complex if children only respect the belt for punishment, and schools are not allowed to touch children.

On the other hand, you have to play the hand you're dealt. African American youth in poverty are just as brilliant as other children, but racist and ignorant teachers have not learned how to teach them. The problem is systemic. In addition, since the *Brown vs. Topeka* decision in 1954, there has been a 66 percent decline in African American teachers, the very teachers who, theoretically, should understand the mindset of African American children in poverty.

Ruby Payne's Position

I was once told by a Minneapolis school faculty that the children lacked discipline. I didn't accept their premise just as I don't accept Ruby Payne's premise. I suggested that we videotape several classes and then have a workshop at the end of the day to review what went on.

The video proved enlightening. The students we followed had "selective discipline." Depending on the teacher, they were either on task or they were all over the classroom. Remember, I was brought in because the children lacked discipline. Imagine how the staff felt when in two of the four classroom periods videotaped the children were focused, on task, and disciplined. They were not disciplined in the other two classrooms.

On the cover of my book *Black Students, Middle-Class Teachers* there is a White female teacher and a Black boy. Eighty-three percent of elementary school teachers are White and female. I spend almost three days a week with White females who are interested in improving their skills, not understanding poverty.

The future of the Black race literally lies in the hands of White female teachers.

What I observed in Minneapolis is occurring throughout the country. Of the two classes in which the children were focused, one had a White female teacher and the other had a Black teacher. In the two classes where the kids were bouncing off the walls, one had a White teacher and the other a Black teacher. So the race card could not be played. Nor could the poverty card.

This variance in student behavior was not because of the race of the teacher or income of the home. There was only one variable and that was the teacher's classroom management skills.

Mother's Level of Education

Ruby Payne says that **the educational level of mothers is the most important influence on the educational attainment of children.** I wholeheartedly disagree. I would encourage Ruby Payne and all those who believe that to read the work of James Comer who has done excellent work in developing the Comer school model. I would also encourage them to read Reginald Clark's book *Family Life and School Achievement* and *Gifted Hands* by Ben Carson. Dr. Carson is considered the best pediatric neurosurgeon in the country. By the way, he grew up in a low-income household, fatherless, and Sonya Carson, his mother, only had a third-grade education.

I'm not trying to glamorize illiteracy and lack of education. At the outset, I said I want to see all of our children in affluent homes with their fathers present and their mothers at home with graduate degrees.

It's not enough to do research and theorize. We must use the findings to develop and implement effective programs. We must take action. Take the case of Head Start and Maxine Waters, the U.S. congresswoman. She began her career humbly, as a Head Start parent, and she lacked a good education. Head Start encouraged her to go to college, which she did. She became a teacher's assistant, a teacher, and a director. Later she went on to the State House of Representatives, the State Senate, and the U.S. Congress. If Ruby Payne or any other person believes that the most important factor is the educational background of the mother, then all of America's resources should be allocated to correct this problem.

(It is amazing how we can find billions of dollars to wage war against Iraq but can finance only 40 percent of the children who qualify to attend Head Start.)

To break the cycle of welfare, a coordinated effort among government agencies, community institutions, churches, and schools is required. In his book *Make A Difference: A Spectacular Breakthrough in the Fight Against Poverty* Gary MacDougal writes that government agencies need to work together to provide transportation, child care, medical benefits, and counseling to empower mothers to reach their full potential. You can't take welfare away and not provide a coordinated strategy to address these issues.

If schools believe that the educational background of the mother is the most important factor, then every school in low-income areas should take a cue from Head Start and provide parent rooms, parent coordinators, computer literacy classes, GED training, and everything else necessary to correct this problem.

Ruby Payne says that poverty is caused by interrelated factors: parents' employment status and earnings, family structure, and parent education. I believe capitalism creates poverty. Poverty is caused by the richest country in the world not providing a livable minimum wage. You can't take care of a family of four with minimum wage. Forty-eight million Americans who work also lack health care and basic benefits. Yet the CEOs of major corporations receive millions of dollars per year in cash, benefits, perks, stock options, pension packages, and more.

One of the largest companies in the world, Wal-Mart, fights against paying workers a livable wage, health care, and pension benefits. In America, 1 percent of the population owns 57 percent of the wealth while 10 percent owns 86 percent of the wealth. That is the reason for poverty. There are few countries in the world with a more unequal distribution of wealth than America. You can't get to the root of the problem by tending the leaves. In Mark 11, Jesus cursed the fig tree at the root. If a person has cancer, the best therapy I believe is not chemo or radiation but building the immune system gets to the root of the problem.

Physical Violence

Ruby Payne believes that *fighting and physical violence are factors of poverty.* She says that the middle class uses space to deal with conflict and disagreements. In the chapter on White poverty, we will look at the 24 million Whites who live below the poverty line. Many people are not aware that there are more Whites who live in poverty than African Americans. The difference is that poor Whites are scattered, and they often live in rural areas, trailer homes, or Section 8 housing in the suburbs.

Thanks to racism and poor government planning, African Americans were placed on top of each other in projects, and it is this face of poverty that has been on the nightly news. Research has shown that if you put thousands of people in one dilapidated building, there will be disharmony. I'm glad to see that more and more cities are demolishing their old housing developments. If it didn't work with rats, why would they think it would work with humans?

Ruby, housing patterns might better explain gangs, crime, and violence than poverty.

Remember the Million Man March in 1995 and the Million More March in 2005? Let's focus on the former since it consisted of all men. The assumption is that if you have more than a million men together in a tight space, there will be fighting. I told my wife that the safest place for any Black male to be on October 16, 1995, was the Million Man March. We stepped on each other, we brushed up against each other, but there were no fights, no murders, no crime that day—and the media and Ruby Payne were silent.

14

Ruby Payne's Position

What made those men behave differently? Was it because they were all millionaires, all members of the middle and upper classes? No. It was because these men knew *whose* men they were; they had a relationship with God. They also knew *who* they were. They understood their history and culture. Why do Black men fight Black men? Why do Black men kill Black men? Is it because they are poor? No. It is because they hate themselves. Why do they hate themselves? Because they have not been taught their history and culture.

Ruby Payne, fighting and gangs could be reduced in schools and neighborhoods if every Black child learned about the Willie Lynch letter. This letter was written to slave owners to teach Africans to look for differences, destroy unity, and teach racial hatred. (The letter can be found on page 85.) Just as every American student must study the U.S. Constitution to pass eighth grade, every African American student should read, write about, discuss, debate, and analyze the Willie Lynch letter and its implications on our community.

In the last chapter, we will look at the importance of Africentricity in the curriculum. The African values of Nguzo Saba and Maat can correct the problem of self-hatred, regardless of income.

Ruby Payne believes that poverty leads to criminal behavior. If poverty is the major contributor to crime, how do we explain white-collar crime? How do we explain Mafia crime? A person steals a candy bar and it's his third offense and he's jailed for life, but a white-collar criminal embezzles $10 billion and is given a $50,000 fine. How do we explain this discrepancy? White-collar crime has a ten times greater impact on society than the petty crimes of stealing VCRs and hubcaps.

The rumor is that there is a war on drugs in America. If that were true, we should go after drug and gun manufacturers or go after drug users, not petty drug dealers. Let me be clear. Affluent communities have a prostitution problem. They don't lock up Jane. If you lock up the petty seller, she will either post bail or her replacement will be on the same corner before the police can bat an eye. Affluent communities that are serious about eliminating prostitution don't go after the seller. They go after the buyer, the user, the John. Jane can't sell if John can't use.

If America were serious about a war on drugs, we would be going after the 74 percent of drug users in America who, for some strange reason, Ruby Payne, are White. How do we explain that Blacks and Latinos are only 26 percent of drug users but constitute more than 70 percent of those convicted for drug possession?

How do we explain, Ruby Payne, that if you have 499 grams of cocaine, the original drug, you get a slap on the wrist and a homework assignment, but 5 grams of derivative crack cocaine means a mandatory sentence?

No, Ruby Payne, I do not agree that poverty is the major contributor to crime. All we have to do is look at the recent Enron scandal. No, crime is driven more by greed than poverty.

Noise Factor

According to Ruby Payne, *there is a high noise level in impoverished communities*. The television is always on at the house, along with the radio and/or CD player. In the classroom, children are always speaking simultaneously. This is true, but I don't agree that "noise" has to be a determining factor in academic performance.

Ruby Payne's Position

In African culture there's a practice called "call and response," and it is prevalent in churches, concerts, storefront
lectures, protest marches, and one-on-one conversations. In
White culture, the audience is expected to be absolutely silent
to hear the performer. There's a separation between the performer and the audience. In Black culture, there is no separation, and this fact transcends income level. The audience and
the performer are one and the same. African American musicians
will tell you they get their energy from the audience. It helps
them with their performance. The same thing happens in the
church. While the preacher is speaking, the congregation encourages him on, and that's called call and response. This transcends poverty.

There have been numerous studies about the two most
popular television shows for children, *Mr. Rogers* and *Sesame
Street*. White children respond better to *Mr. Rogers* which is
very slow; Black and Hispanic children respond to *Sesame
Street* which is much faster. The rumor is that Black and Hispanic children are hyperactive. In order to label someone hyper
you have to know what normal activity is. Who has the right
to define what's normal for African Americans? Only African
Americans. The energy level of our children may be higher
than that of others. This is strength, not weakness. People
who believe in the cultural deficit model feel that what they do
is correct. There's a distinction between being different and
being deficient.

Many educators believe that the ideal student is one who
can sit still for long periods of time, quietly working by himself
on ditto sheets that lie about Columbus discovering America.
The unfortunate reality is that if a child cannot sit still for long
periods of time, he may be labeled ADD (Attention Deficit
Disorder) or ADHD (Attention Deficit Hyperactivity Disorder), and a prescription of Ritalin will not be far behind.

17

If I were a classroom teacher, I would much rather have 30 active students who are blurting out the answer because they are so excited about the information than to have 30 zombies who are not saying anything.

Ujamaa (Cooperative Economics)

Ruby Payne believes that *one of the hidden rules of poverty is that extra money is shared.* On one hand, I pray she is correct. I pray that in the Black community, African Americans are sharing their money. Last year we earned $723 billion. I pray that African Americans are taking care of the homeless, the needy, tithing to their churches, contributing to the United Negro College Fund and many other worthwhile causes. I don't see anything wrong with that.

The issue that Ruby Payne raises here is that schools teach more than the three Rs. They teach values. If schools teach students to value *me* and not *we*, competition over cooperation, then how will African American students, who value cooperation, fare in such an environment? For many African American and Hispanic youth, there is a cultural problem here. For example, being the only African American in AP, honors, or gifted and talented classes is not always an honor because it means friends are being left behind. African American students tend not to see this as a competitive win but a loss of camaraderie and support. Schools are insensitive to African American children feeling uncomfortable in those kinds of environments.

To put the shoe on the other foot, Ruby Payne, how would a White student feel in an all Black environment where the students are either openly hostile or coldly polite? They'd feel uncomfortable, too.

Ruby Payne's Position

Many schools are concerned not only about the few African American students in advanced classes but the performance of those that have made the grade. Often, African American students don't do as well as expected. I always encourage schools in this predicament to be even more aggressive about increasing the number of African American students in advanced classes. If the number of students increases, performance will improve.

In sixth grade, I learned a lesson I never will forget. My teacher, Mrs. Butler, asked me what my math grade was. I said 100. She said, "What about your best friend Darrell?" I snickered. She then told me to bring my paper to her desk, and she asked me another question: "What grade did Darrell receive?" I said 40. She then drew an X through my 100 and wrote 40. She said, "From now on, whatever grade Darrell receives will also be yours."

You may think that was unfair, but from an African perspective, "I am because we are." The European perspective believes that "I" is more important than "we." Competition is more important than cooperation. Mrs. Butler taught me more than math that year. She taught me values.

So Ruby Payne, it's good that many African Americans have a desire to share. I just pray that you're correct, because I'm concerned that more and more African Americans are adopting the American value system of "I have mine and you have yours to get." I'm especially concerned about the "middle class" that has moved out of the "poverty arena" and has forgotten from whence they came. If anything, I wish the middle class and the upper class had some of the same values that you see in the "lower class."

The Value of Education

Ruby Payne believes that *education is the key for getting out of and staying out of generational poverty.* In the chapter on race and integration, we will explore whether this statement is true or not. We will document the findings of race testers who, among other things, found that a White male felon with only a high school diploma earns more money than an African American male with a college degree and no prison record.

Ruby Payne, you can't talk about poverty if you're not going to talk about racism and capitalism. Those are the two major factors that contribute to poverty.

In the next chapter, we will look at White poverty. This group is marginalized in our society. They are victims, not of racism, but of capitalism.

CHAPTER 2: WHITE POVERTY

The National Center for Children and Poverty, along with the U.S. Census Department, defines poverty as follows:

$20,000 or less for a family of four
$16,600 or less for a family of three
$13,200 for a family of two
$10,000 for a single person.

I often ask students, "How many poor people do you think live in America?"

Now, reader, I want to ask you the same question. How many poor people live in America? How many poor people are White? Black? Hispanic? Asian? Native American?

There are 40 million Americans who live below the poverty line in the richest country in the world. The reality is that the 40 million figure is rising and has been every year. Listed below are the numbers of people living below the poverty line based on race or ethnicity.

20 million Whites
9 million African Americans
9 million Hispanics
2 million Asians/Native Americans

Most students are shocked to learn that of the 40 million poor people in America, 50 percent, or 20 million, are White. Interestingly, very little of Ruby Payne's theories are directed toward the 20 million Whites who live below the poverty line. Ten percent of all White children in America live below the poverty line. There are almost 10 million White children who live below the poverty line, and Ruby Payne is silent.

What are her theories about poor White families? What are her strategies for 10 million White children living below the poverty line? How is she helping teachers to better understand White children who live below the poverty line? What strategies is she offering to the millions of White parents whose children live below the poverty line?

The media, electronic and print, have also been silent about White poverty. Most of us are dependent on electronic media for our information. Unless we seek out alternative sources of information, we will never hear the truth about American poverty.

The last images that we saw of White poverty, and this was before the tremendous advancement of television, were during the Great Depression of the 1930s. We saw large numbers of Whites distraught, committing suicide, and waiting in food lines during the Depression.

During the early 1960s, there were many media specials and documentaries on poverty, but only 25 percent of those studies examined poverty in the African American community. However, in the 1970s, 75 percent of all media reports on welfare and poverty emphasized and portrayed the African American community. What caused this shift in focus? Why do the media ignore half the population that lives below the poverty line? Why is Ruby Payne so silent about 20 million Whites who live below the poverty line, 10 million of whom are children?

America is the richest country in the world, and that may partially explain why the media and Ruby Payne are so silent about White poverty. This is an embarrassment to "First World" America. Look at how poverty in America compares to poverty in other rich industrial countries.

White Poverty

Percent of Children in Poverty

1.6 Sweden
2.8 Germany
4.6 France
7.4 United Kingdom
9.3 Canada
20.4 United States

What is it about America that allows 20 percent of its children to live below the poverty line? What makes Sweden, Germany, France, the United Kingdom, and Canada better than the U.S. in this area? Do any of Ruby Payne's theories explain why America ranks so low in child poverty?

In the deficit theory model, the problem is with the victim, not the system or institutions. We're talking about 20 million Whites who live in a country of White privilege, who in spite of White supremacy are not able to rise above the poverty level. Is that why the country is embarrassed? Does that explain why the media is silent? Could it be that Ruby Payne does not have any theories to eradicate White poverty because White America is in denial of 20 million Whites who live below the poverty line?

Who advocates for this group? What programs are being developed and offered to empower 20 million poor Whites? Historically, in 1619, Africans were not slaves. They were indentured servants along with poor Whites. But White America found it difficult to maintain and identify the less fortunate whether they were White or Black.

From 1620, African Americans were no longer indentured servants. Unlike White indentured servants who could work their way out of servitude, African Americans were literally confined to slavery from birth to death. In the next chapter on racism and Black poverty, we will elaborate on the differences between White poverty and Black poverty, but in this chapter, we're trying to understand why it is so difficult for 20 million Whites to rise above the poverty line, much less reach the low-income category in a country of White privilege.

Earlier I used the term "First World." Words are powerful. If there is a First World, there has to be a Second, a Third, etc. What makes America first? First in divorce, homicide, suicide, incarceration, and first in the widest differential of income and wealth.

In America, 1 percent of the population owns 57 percent of the wealth. Ten percent owns 86 percent of the wealth. Only 14 percent of America's wealth is available to 90 percent of the population.

Ruby Payne, if we're going to be serious about eradicating poverty, we need to address the imbalance in the distribution of wealth in America. Is it fair that 90 percent of the population only has 14 percent of America's wealth? If we are serious about empowering students, then our curricula should look at how we can better distribute the wealth so that 20 percent of America's children do not need to live below the poverty line.

I resent going into an educational institution that insists on discussing poverty. Notice I said discuss it, not eradicate it. Let's discuss how poverty prevents us from being effective educators. If poverty and economics mean that much to us, then let's become serious about looking for ways to distribute the wealth more equitably.

What is even more unfortunate is that the 20 million poor Whites believe they have more in common with the 10 percent that controls 86 percent of the wealth. This flawed thinking goes all the way back to 1620. The slave owner convinced the White indentured servant that his lowly status was still better than the slave's. White privilege kept him from that fate worse than death. Therefore, if you stick with us, the masters said, while you may not be able to live in a great mansion that sits on a hundred acres of land, at least you'll be better than an African slave.

I never will forget the senatorial election in North Carolina that pitted Jesse Helms against Harvey Gant. Gant had an agenda for poor Whites living in North Carolina, but Jesse Helms was able to convince them that it was better to vote for a White regardless of his policy than to vote for a Black man.

In the last presidential election, it was difficult for the Democrats to win the South because poor Whites have been taught that it is better to vote and identify with the White ruling class than to identify with poor African Americans and Hispanics.

It is usually low-income and impoverished communities that suffer racial tension, not affluent communities. The 10 percent ruling class has decided they don't have a problem with African Americans moving into their neighborhood—as long as they have $5 million to purchase a home. As a result of that requirement, they have reduced, if not eliminated, the number of African Americans that can move into certain neighborhoods.

In contrast, when African Americans and Hispanics move to poor White neighborhoods where there are fewer economic restrictions, hostilities almost always occur. Martin Luther King had been beaten, cursed, and thrown into jails by hostile Southern Whites, but he said he had never seen such racism, such venom, and such hatred as when he marched in Gage Park, a Southwest Side neighborhood in Chicago. Much more will be said about integration in a later chapter.

It is unfortunate that the media emphasize African American poverty. Laziness is one of the stereotypes attached to the

African American poor. This argument has always amazed me. If African Americans were so lazy, why did Whites travel three months on a slave ship to Africa and three months back to America to bring home lazy people? If Whites were so industrious, had such a strong work ethic, why didn't they do the work themselves? At least they could have used their indentured servants to build up the country.

This belief parallels the theory that poverty is the major reason for the academic achievement gap. This is a "blame the victim" mentality. How do we reconcile and rationalize 20 million Whites living below the poverty line in a country of White privilege? Are the 20 million poor Whites lazy? Did their schools fail them? Did capitalism exploit them?

In American capitalism, "full" employment is defined as 4 percent being unemployed. How do we explain that? If full means all, then every person who wants to work is employed. Full employment should equate to 100 percent.

But if everyone were employed, then capitalists would not have leverage over the workers. Wages would rise. As long as a percentage of the population is unemployed, the capitalists can keep wages low. Capitalism exploits all workers, including those of White privilege.

Schools reflect our capitalistic economy. The economy requires a few to make decisions and the majority to do menial work. If every student had a Ph.D., the economy would have no one to clean the buildings and work at Wal-Mart and McDonalds. These are the growth areas for workers. Tracking students allows schools to produce winners and losers. The winners attend advanced placement, honors, and gifted and talented. The losers attend remedial and special education. Schools should teach students how to eradicate poverty in our nation. I challenge Ruby Payne and her advocates who are

White Poverty

serious about the issue of poverty to develop strategies for reducing poverty among 20 million Whites.

Maybe the reason why the media does not focus on White poverty is because they don't know where poor Whites reside. Maybe it's easier to send out a cameraman and a reporter to an urban high rise 20 blocks from the station to do a quick report on how difficult it is to live in a building that was designed for 5,000 but is being occupied by 25,000 people, a building where the heat and air conditioning are inadequate if available at all. Elevators are malfunctioning, and recreation and employment programs are nonexistent. I guess it's easier for the producer to send his staff to the high rise than to seek out the impoverished. Where are the poor Whites? They are in rural America, the mountains, trailer parks, and scattered-site housing in suburbia.

I wonder how much time Ruby Payne spends in rural America, the mountains, trailer homes, and scattered-site housing. Forty-four percent of White Americans who live in rural areas are poor. It's easy for the media and Ruby Payne to identify poor African Americans because 75 percent live in neighborhoods where more than 20 percent of the residents are poor. In contrast, only 25 percent of poor Whites live in neighborhoods where 20 percent or more of the residents are poor.

It's easy for the media and Ruby Payne to identify Black poverty because it is so concentrated and visible.

I would love for Ruby Payne and her advocates to explain why Black poverty is more concentrated than White poverty. What are the implications of poor people living in such densely populated areas? What are the benefits of poor people living in neighborhoods that are less concentrated with poverty? I am reminded of the pre-integration era in Black America when the Black haves and have-nots lived in the same neighborhood, where someone on ADC lived next door to someone who possessed a Ph.D. I wonder how living next door to a doctor influenced a poor child.

I encourage everyone reading this book to take a trip through poor White America. You need to visit the South, especially states like West Virginia and Tennessee. All of Ruby Payne's advocates should visit rural America, the mountains, trailer homes, and scattered Section 8 housing in White suburbs.

It is interesting and ironic that rural America has found an economic growth industry called prisons. African Americans are only 12 percent of the U.S. population, but they constitute more than 50 percent of all U.S. inmates. More than 60 percent of all prison inmates are there because of drug-related crimes and many governors correlate prison growth with fourth-grade reading scores.[6]

If the prisons are being populated by large numbers of African Americans from urban areas, why are the prisons being built in rural America? Why do rural towns literally fight over who's going to receive the next prison? Is this the only way America knows how to employ poor White males? Does this further explain why prisons have dropped the word "rehabilitation" and why we now have a recidivism rate of 85 percent while spending $28,000 per inmate per year? Does it further extend and exacerbate the tension between poor Whites and poor Blacks that White prison guards without degrees earn more money than teachers with degrees?

Can Ruby Payne help us understand the dichotomy between urban poverty and rural poverty? Does she have a theory to help us understand how poor Whites and poor Blacks are being exploited by the 10 percent ruling class? Does she offer the 20 million poor Whites that deserve better any empowerment strategies?

In the next chapter, we will look at the population Ruby Payne focuses most of her attention on—African Americans.

CHAPTER 3: BLACK POVERTY

I believe numbers can tell a story. When I speak to groups, I use an overhead projector and screen or PowerPoint presentation to show audiences the story I am trying to tell with numbers. For example, the following numbers tell the story of the economic status of African Americans.

36 million African Americans live in the United States.
9 million African Americans live below the poverty line.
25 percent of African Americans live below the poverty line.
33 percent of African American children live below the poverty line.
50 percent of African American children are either low income or below the poverty line.
50 percent of African American families earn between $20,000 and $50,000 per year.
25 percent of African American families earn more than $50,000 per year.

Let's now review these numbers and see what they are telling us. In the previous chapter, we mentioned that 20 million Whites live below the poverty line compared to 9 million African Americans. From an aggregate perspective, there are more Whites below the poverty line than African Americans—20 million to 9 million. From a percentage perspective, 25 percent of African Americans live below the poverty line and only 10 percent of Whites.

Thirty-three percent of African American children live below the poverty line compared to only 10 percent of White children. Unfortunately, a large percentage of African American children who live below the poverty line are concentrated in densely populated urban areas and have inadequate housing. This is in contrast to the 10 million White children who are distributed in rural areas, mountain regions, trailer homes, and scattered-site housing.

Not only do the media focus on a smaller number of African American families and children who live below the poverty line, they also make the Black family monolithic. While 25 percent of Black families live below the poverty line, another 25 percent earn more than $50,000 per year. Sixteen percent of African American families earn more than $100,000 per year. But those two percentages do not exceed the larger figure of 50 percent, that group which earns between $20,000 and $50,000. The Black family is not monolithic. Yet, when you read the work of Ruby Payne, it's as if she's speaking of a monolithic community.

Which Black family are you talking about? The 25 percent below the poverty line, the 25 percent who earn more than $50,000 per year, or the 50 percent in the middle?

Remember the African American family portrayed in the *Cosby Show*? It featured Claire and Cliff Huxtable, a doctor and a lawyer. Many thought this upper-income family was unrealistic, an anomaly. In reality, this occurs 25 percent of the time in the African American family.

In TV land there are three types of Black families. *Good Times* represented the first 25 percent, *Roc* the 50 percent middle group, and the *Cosby Show* the upscale 25 percent.

Ruby Payne, the Black family is not monolithic.

The most important chart in this chapter is listed below.

Black Poverty

Ratio of black to white wealth and income

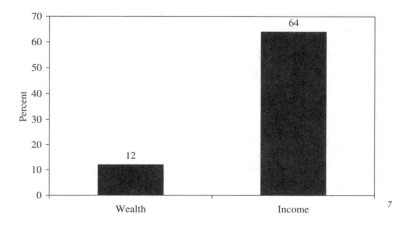

7

Let's review what this chart teaches us. The average White family earns $44,000 in income compared to only $28,000 for African American families. African Americans earn 64 percent of White income. Ironically, this is close to how the Constitution defined Blacks over 200 years ago, that is, as being three-fifths of a person. If you review the Black-White income ratio for the past 40 years, it shows the consistency of racism. The Black-White income differential has fluctuated between 55 and 65 percent—close to 60 percent, or three-fifths of a person.

There is a tremendous distinction between income and wealth. In the next chapter on economic empowerment, we will look at that in more detail. Since Ruby Payne is so concerned about poverty, I would like her to teach African American children and the teachers who work with them the distinction between income and wealth.

For example, there are two families who both earn $40,000 in income, but that does not mean they will have the same amount of wealth. If you look at the above chart, the wealth gap far exceeds the income gap. The average White family has $67,000 in wealth compared to only $8,000 in wealth for African Americans. While we are 36 percent short in income, we are 88 percent short in wealth.

Earlier we mentioned the poor distribution of wealth in America. One percent of America's population owns 57 percent of the wealth, and 10 percent owns 86 percent of the wealth. While the above figures of $67,000 and $8,000 are averages, there are large numbers of White and Black families who have no wealth at all.

Why do 25 percent of African Americans live below the poverty line? Why do 33 percent of African American children live below the poverty line? Are they lazy? Are they culturally deprived of middle-class values? Do they need to be taught the theories of Ruby Payne to move them out of poverty?

In the book *Minority Education and Caste,* the late John Ogbu answers Ruby Payne and her advocates:

Predictably, the remedial programs generated by these theories do not focus on eliminating Black subordination and exclusion as a way of eliminating their academic retardation. Instead they focus on rehabilitating individual Blacks from the supposed bad influences of their families and communities on their development of school-related skills. This is essentially a conservative approach. Schools translate the inferior social and techno-economic status of Blacks into inferior education that caste barriers do not permit Blacks to translate their academic skills into good jobs, income, and other benefits. These conditions result in Blacks developing attitudes and skills less favorable to White middle-class values. Therefore, the lower school performance of blacks is not itself the central problem but an expression of a more fundamental one, mainly caste barriers and the ideology that supports them. The elimination of caste barriers is the only lasting solution to the problem of academic retardation. Programs that seek to change school policies and practices and to help Blacks develop new attitudes and skills are necessary but auxiliary components of this strategy cannot by themselves prove effective in solving the problem of school failure among caste-like minorities in the United States.[8]

Ruby Payne, we need to address the root issue rather than attempt to use the deficit model to fix Black children. The fundamental issue here pertains not just to Black children in poverty but also to White children in poverty. Capitalism and classism have created poverty in the richest country in the world.

Earlier we documented that regardless of race, people suffer from classism and capitalism. In the case of the African American community, we not only need to look at the impact of class and capitalism, but we must also look at racism.

Ruby Payne, can you and your proponents say the word "racism"? Can you say "White supremacy"? These are the reasons why African Americans earn 64 percent of White income. Racism and White supremacy are the major reasons why there is an 88 percent disparity between White and Black wealth.

Free Labor

Let's now look historically at what happened to African Americans in this country so that we can properly document and explain why such a large portion of the African American community languishes in its current state. This did not happen overnight.

More than eight million Africans and their descendants were enslaved in the United States from 1620 to 1865. The practice of slavery constituted an immoral and inhuman deprivation of Africans' life and liberty and African citizenship rights, cultural heritage, and the fruit of their own labor. Historians estimate that one slave perished for every one who survived capture in the African interior and made it alive to the New World. As many as 12 million perished along the way. Some historians estimate that as many as 100 million Africans died between 1620 and 1865, if you include Africa, the Caribbean, Central and South America, and North America. A more accurate estimate is that more than 30 million Africans died in the slave trade.

In 1786, the framers of the Constitution laid the legal foundation for a Black-White wealth and power imbalance by counting Blacks as three-fifths of a person. More than 31 percent of the delegates to the Philadelphia Constitutional Convention were slaveholders, who together owned approximately 1400 slaves. The framers were idealists, but they were also racists.

James Madison and George Washington were two of the more prosperous delegates to the convention. Their capital investment in slaves would be valued at approximately $105 million today. The delegates were protecting their slave investments and the nation's free labor system. They believed that Black slave labor was necessary for the development of the nation and the prosperity of Whites in this country.

34

Black Poverty

Ruby Payne and her proponents should talk about the origins of African American poverty and dissect what happened between 1620 and 1865. The following chart illustrates the significance of slavery and the wealth it provided for the White community and the poverty it created for the Black community.

Year	Average Slave Price
1800	$600
1810	$900
1820	$1050
1840	$1200
1860	$1600
1862	$1800

Claud Anderson, in the powerful book *Black Labor, White Wealth,* said,

Land ownership, Whites' second great source of wealth, did not surpass slave ownership as the primary form of wealth accumulation until well after the Civil War. The profitability of Black slaves as a wealth-producing commodity was so great that anything short of a Civil War would have had little if any affect on the slavery system. The $7 billion capital investment in Black slaves in 1860 exceeded all other business investments in the North, South, and Federal budget combined. The nation's wealth was in the South. Two out of three males with $100,000 personal net worth lived in the South and owned slaves. The wealth accumulation of the typical cotton belt farm was four times greater than that of the usual Northern farmer and was 91 times greater than that of the typical urban common laborer. On average, the large Southern plantation owners who used slave gang systems had 18 times more wealth than a Northern farmer and nearly 400 times more wealth than the average Northern urban laborer.[9]

Slavery fueled the prosperity of the United States. From 1790 to 1860 alone, the U.S. economy reaped the benefits by as much as $40 million in unpaid labor. Some estimate the current value of this unpaid labor at $1.4 trillion. We will discuss this in more detail in the next chapter.

Ruby Payne, let's talk about reparations. If you're serious about addressing poverty, then you and your proponents need to teach African American youth how to calculate the cost of their ancestors' labor between 1619 and 1865 and the wealth it created for America. It is amazing how people who want to discuss poverty cannot say the words "racism," "White supremacy," or "reparations."

Homestead Act of 1862
Why do African Americans only earn 64 percent of White income? Why is there an 88 percent deficit in the wealth between Whites and Blacks? One reason is the Homestead Act of 1862, which represented America's last great land policy. It was enacted on the eve of the Civil War and provided that anyone

living on land for five years while making some improvements could acquire a free title to 160 acres. This act was unavailable to African Americans. This Act remained in effect until 1900 and provided 400,000 to 600,000 White families with homes and farms. By 1900, most of the land had gone to speculators who thus acquired the claims to rich Western lands, timber, and mineral rights without having to bid or compete for the wealth.

The Gold Rush

Why is there such a wide disparity in income and wealth, Ruby Payne? National race-based economic preferences were used to tie up the California gold fields for Whites. The two groups who contributed the most to building the new nation—Indians with their land and Blacks with their labor—were systematically excluded from participating in the gold rush. In an effort to keep the California gold rush a "White only treasure hunt," public pronouncements made it clear to free Blacks and Indians that if they wanted to pan gold, they could only do it as a slave to a White person. The hundreds of free Blacks who traveled to California in search of gold were in for a rude awakening. They were blocked by local laws and White vigilante violence. California was one of the few free states, so Blacks forced out of the gold fields had few other places to go. Most starved to death, were lynched, or died from exposure.

Let us be clear. There was a tremendous free transfer of land to Whites. African Americans were prevented from taking advantage of the gold rush. After the Civil War Africans were promised 40 acres, a mule, and—people often forget—$50. They did not receive any of that. In spite of all this, however, the African will to survive has been tremendous. Case in point: Tulsa, Oklahoma.

The Black community in North Tulsa was called "Little Africa" by local White newspapers and included the Black business district, referred to as "Black Wall Street." The district was called Black Wall Street because more than 600 Black-owned businesses flourished, including banks and oil, insurance, and real estate companies. Lawyers and doctors, libraries, hospitals, hotels, schools, theaters, and restaurants flourished.

Tulsa, Oklahoma, was not an anomaly. Similar communities arose in almost every Southern state, where African Americans organized themselves, regardless of the lack of capital, to try to develop themselves. An excellent parallel to North Tulsa was in Durham, North Carolina. It was called the Hayti District.

In the spring of 1921 a war broke out in Tulsa. Hundreds were killed and wounded on both sides. The conflict stemmed from an armed standoff over the attempted lynching of a Black man who was, after the battle, proven innocent of assaulting a White woman. White mobs began to attack Blacks individually. The Black community was bombed by the U.S. military, the KKK, and the National Guard. Thousands of Whites looted Black homes and set them on fire. More than 10,000 Black people were left homeless.

If we're serious about understanding Black poverty, then every American history book needs to teach all students about what happened in Tulsa, Oklahoma, in 1921. But just as America is silent about racism, White supremacy, and reparations, the books are also silent about Tulsa, Oklahoma.

As an educational consultant, I often work with teachers who tell me that they don't see color. They see children as children. I'm always amazed that they can look me in the eye (I'm six feet tall and African American) and tell me that they don't see color. When I visit their classrooms I see a multicultural student body, but the bulletin boards, library collections, and posters all reflect *Dick and Jane* Eurocentrism. Yet these are the same teachers who say they don't see color.

Another way we can understand Black poverty in America is through the prism of racial testers. Slavery and the bombing of Black Tulsa are from our long-term memories. Let me share with you some recent results from racial testers.

A field experiment was conducted by the Massachusetts Institute of Technology and the University of Chicago. They sent out 5,000 resumes in response to help wanted ads in Boston and Chicago newspapers. Each resume was randomly assigned either a very Black sounding name, such as L'Keisha Washington or Jamal Jones, or a very White sounding name, such as Emily Walsh or Brendan Baker.

This racial indicator, the researchers found, produced a significant gap in the rate of callbacks for interviews. White names received roughly 50 percent more callbacks than Black names. White applicants, moreover, sending higher-quality resumes, increased the number of callbacks by 30 percent. For Black names, higher-quality resumes elicited no significant callback premium.

In an academic study conducted by Northwestern University sociologist Devah Pager in Milwaukee, Wisconsin, the possession of a prison record reduced the likelihood of White testers being called back by a prospective employer by a ratio of two to one. Among Black testers, the mark of a prison record reduced that likelihood by nearly three to one.

Two legal foundations sued Watertower Surgicenter. The Legal Assistance Foundation of Chicago sent two sets of female employment testers, one White and one Black, to Watertower to apply for a receptionist position. In both cases

39

the Black job seekers were discouraged by the human resources director after submitting resumes and completing the application. Neither Black tester was formally interviewed or tested for the job. The less qualified White testers were immediately given clerical and typing tests, trained on the phone system, introduced to other employees, and then offered the position.

In the study titled "Race and Work," testers applied to 1470 actual entry-level jobs throughout New York City. The study carefully tracked and matched teams of testers, interviews, and resultant job offers. As a result, they were able to explicitly identify patterns of discrimination in New York City's low-wage labor markets and dispute popular conceptions that racial inequalities and intolerances are relics of a bygone era.

Overall, White job applicants were found to be treated more respectfully during interviews than Blacks and were much more consistently offered employment than their fellow testers. The study discovered that Blacks are only slightly more than half as likely to receive consideration by employers as equally qualified White applicants. Further discoveries were made when testers introduced evidence of a previous felony conviction. Although positive responses for Whites declined significantly, they still managed to remain higher than those of Black applicants with *no* presentation of felony convictions. White felon applicants received a 13 percent positive response and Blacks with no criminal record, a 10 percent positive response rate.

Finally, recent work examined the practice of "channeling" applicants to particular positions if they would be willing to consider a different position of greater or lesser responsibility and/or pay scale. Out of a total of 96 channeling cases encountered by testers, Black applicants were channeled downward to lower-level jobs in 10 cases. In no case was a Black applicant channeled upward to a higher-level position. Whites, and only those indicating a criminal history, encountered downward channeling only four times.

Earlier we mentioned the discrimination based on African names. We have also seen discrimination based on the hue of African Americans. A light-skinned African American has a 50 percent better chance of getting a job than a dark-skinned African American. I would encourage Ruby Payne and her proponents to look into the concepts of "good hair" and "pretty eyes." Observe classrooms where teachers have light-skinned children sitting in the front and dark-skinned children sitting in the rear, where light-skinned children are called on more than dark-skinned children, and where teachers have higher expectations of light-skinned children. Don't think this kind of discrimination is simply a relic of the past.

Historically we know that the reason for this hue distinction was based on the fact that Thomas Jefferson couldn't get enough of Sally Hemmings at night. The offspring of White male slave owners and Black women worked in the house while the other Africans worked in the field. That created a schism between house Negroes and field Negroes, between light-skinned African Americans and dark-skinned African Americans.

There was a time when some Black colleges and sororities would only admit light-skinned African Americans. As a result of this kind of discrimination, not only do light-skinned African Americans have a greater chance of securing employment but there's even a difference in the overall income levels between light-skinned and dark-skinned African Americans. I wonder if Ruby Payne knows about the brown bag test. If you were darker than the bag you were not admitted to certain sororities or colleges.

Ruby Payne and her proponents are silent about this phenomenon in the Black community that historically has been perpetuated by racism.

Ruby Payne believes in the importance of education. One of the reasons John Ogbu felt that the caste system was alive and well in America was because African Americans who do stay in school soon learn there is no assured payoff. Those who finish college have a jobless rate 2.24 times that of Whites with diplomas, and an even greater gap separates Black and White high school graduates. Ruby Payne, African Americans are not quite convinced that an education pays in a racist society.

Another major reason for the income-wealth disparity is the discriminatory practices of the financial industry. Blacks are more likely to receive high-interest mortgage loans than Whites. After analyzing lending data, the Association of Community Organizations for Reform Now found that 32 percent of Blacks received high-interest loans to purchase homes. That number, at 8 percent, was drastically different for Whites. In some cases, minority borrowers with good credit are steered toward high-cost loans more appropriate for borrowers with low credit scores.

Homebuyers who may not qualify for regular mortgages due to blemished credit or other reasons have been able to obtain higher-interest-rate mortgages through the sub-prime industry, which is a fast-growing market. However, when Blacks go to these sub-prime lenders, companies that charge higher interest rates than banks, they are still 30 percent more likely to pay higher mortgage rates than White borrowers with similar credit ratings and income levels.

The *Charlotte Observer* reported that Blacks who borrow from 25 of the nation's largest lenders were four times more likely than Whites to pay high rates. Even Blacks with income above $100,000 per year were charged high rates more often than Whites with incomes below $40,000.

If Ruby Payne and her proponents are serious about eradicating poverty, they need to give workshops to the racist employers we just described. She also needs to provide in-service training to the financial industries that discriminate against African Americans at every income level.

This issue is not just about race. White women are only paid 68 cents for every dollar White men earn. African American women are only paid 63 percent of what White men earn. The average woman is cheated out of about $250,000 in wages over a lifetime.

The AFL-CIO estimates that working families lose $200 billion of income annually to the male-female wage gap. The most popular current theory is that women opt out of the workforce to have children. Those nonworking mothers' nonwages are supposed to bring down women's average wages, but that is not how the wage gap is figured. The wages of women who are staying home with a child or who are working part-time are not counted in the official Labor Department averages. Only full-time workers' wages are computed.

You would think that Ruby Payne, being a female, would be furious about the feminization of poverty. This is even more acute in the African American family, where 68 percent of African American children are being reared in single-parent homes. This feminization of poverty needs to be addressed. In a typical two-parent family, there might be a father with a high school diploma making $20 an hour as a truck driver and a mother with an associate's degree earning $10 an hour as an administrative assistant. Collectively they're bringing in $30 an hour to the family. If they divorce, the mother-headed family loses two-thirds of its income.

Why is the truck driver, with his high school diploma, paid $20 an hour and the administrative assistant, who has a degree and has mastered Microsoft Word, Excel, PowerPoint, and numerous other software programs, only paid $10 an hour? When I was in college, several of my male classmates did not complete the last year of their education because when they crunched the numbers, they realized they could earn more money as a city bus driver, UPS truck driver, or driving for a commercial truck firm than they could with a degree.

Thomas Shapiro tried to explain the income-wealth differences between Blacks and Whites in his book *The Hidden Cost of Being African American.* I would encourage Ruby Payne and her proponents to read it. Shapiro says the income gap has nothing to do with work ethic, education, IQ, laziness, or any other social issue. It has everything to do with accumulated wealth and home ownership. He says that for many Americans, the acquisition of wealth is predicated on home ownership.

Let's say there are two families, one Black and one White. Both earn the same amount of income, but the Black family rents and the White family owns a home. The Black family rents because they do not have any savings to use as a down payment on a home. They may rent for 5, 10, 15, or 20 years before they finally save enough to purchase a home. The White family also had difficulties saving enough for a down payment. The difference is that the White couple received a gift or long-term loan from their parents and/or grandparents, who benefited from the accumulated wealth of past generations. Some newly wed White couples receive homes as wedding presents, and others receive their homes via an inheritance.

Ruby Payne, the accumulated wealth of White families was not created by a lecture on poverty, nor did it come from a strong work ethic. White America benefited from free labor from 1620 to 1865, the Homestead Act, the gold rush, and innumerable examples of economic racism that have occurred over the past 400 years.

I also recommend the brilliant White scholar Andrew Hacker and his book *Two Nations.* Let me close this chapter with a quote from his book.

Most White Americans will say that, all things considered, things aren't so bad for Black people in the United States. What White people seldom stop to ask is how they may benefit from belonging to their race. Let us try to find out by means of a parable and assume that what follows may actually happen: title "The Visit."

You will be visited tonight by an official you have never met. He begins by telling you that he is extremely embarrassed. The organization he represents has made a mistake, something that hardly ever happens. According to their records, he goes on, you were to have been born Black to another set of parents far from where you were raised. However, the rules being what they are, this error must be rectified and as soon as possible. So at midnight tonight, you will become Black. And this will mean not simply a darker skin, but the bodily and facial features associated with African ancestry. However, inside you'll be the person you always were. Your knowledge and ideas will remain intact, but outwardly you will not be recognizable to anyone you now know.

Your visitor empathizes that being born to the wrong parents was in no way your fault. Consequently, his organization is prepared to offer you some reasonable recompense. Would you, he asks, care to name a sum of money you might consider appropriate? He adds that his group is by no means poor. He can be quite generous when the circumstances warrant as they seem to in your case. He finishes by saying that the records show that you are scheduled to live another 50 years as a Black man or woman in America. How much financial recompense do you request? End of story.

When this parable is put to White students, most seem to feel that it would not be out of place to ask for $50 million, or $1 million for each coming Black year. This calculation conveys as well as anything the value that White people place on their own skin. Indeed, to be White is to possess a gift whose value can be appreciated only after it has been taken away. Why ask so large a sum? Surely this needs no detailing. The money would be used as best it could to buy protection from the discrimination and dangers White people know they would face once they were perceived to be Black.[10]

In the next chapter we will look at economic empowerment. If Ruby Payne is that concerned about poverty and its impact on African Americans and their educational achievement, then she should begin to address the root issue, and that's how to economically empower African Americans.

CHAPTER 4: ECONOMIC EMPOWERMENT

The title of Ruby Payne's best seller is *A Framework for Understanding Poverty*. The key word in the title is "poverty." As Robert Woodson said, we have consultants, leaders, and authors who can talk about poverty, consult on poverty, write about poverty, but cannot eradicate or eliminate poverty.

Poverty, like crime, sells. It is a billion-dollar industry. Many social workers and other professionals would be unemployed if they empowered their clients economically or if they created strategies to eliminate poverty. At the outset, I stated that I don't want to study poverty. I want to study what schools and educators have done effectively with low-income children to produce schools and students above the national average.

It is better to teach someone how to fish than to give them a fish. The title of Payne's book leads you down a road that accepts poverty as a fact of African American life that will never go away: we must understand poverty so that we can help the poor educationally. I beg to disagree.

This chapter is interested in looking at a new or different paradigm. Ruby Payne, rather than understanding poverty, why not re-title the book, *A Framework for Understanding Wealth* or *A Framework for Understanding Capitalism* or *A Framework for Understanding Money Management*. Why not give your clients a copy of my book on economics, which is titled *Black Economics: Solutions for Economic Empowerment*.

If you believe, Ruby Payne, that the major reason for the academic achievement gap is poverty, then we can correct that problem by teaching poor people, particularly African Americans, the principles of wealth, money management, and capitalism. Capitalistic countries should mandate schools to teach economic literacy. Before a child graduates from eighth or twelfth grade, they should understand and master the principles of wealth, capitalism, and money management. I commend those few states that have passed legislation requiring their students to take a class in financial literacy. It is possible to graduate from high school and be financially illiterate. The following quiz should be a requirement for every eighth and twelfth grader before they receive their diploma.

Economic Literacy Quiz

What is the difference in cost: cashing a check at a Payday store, currency exchange, or bank?

What is the difference in the rate of return deposited in a bank, savings and loan, money market, mutual fund, or common stock?

What is an income statement, cash flow statement, balance sheet, and cost of goods sold statement?

What is the difference in cost: paying bills with a money order from a currency exchange or a check from a bank?

What is the difference between gross and net sales?

What is the difference between the wholesale and retail price?

What are the implications of a low vs. a high credit score?

Do cars and houses appreciate equally?

What does it mean to pay yourself first?

What is Rule 72?

Ruby Payne, if we're going to discuss poverty, then every student and teacher needs to know the answers to these questions. And reader, how well did you do on the quiz?

Everyone needs to know Rule 72. In my book *Black Economics,* we discuss this in detail.

48

72 ÷ rate of return = # of years for investment to double.

RULE 72		
1%	=	72 years
4%	=	18 years
5%	=	14.4 years
6%	=	12 years
10%	=	7.2 years
12%	=	6 years
18%	=	4 years
24%	=	3 years

At a 12 percent return, $10,000.00 becomes:		
$20,000.00	in	6 years
$40,000.00	in	12 years
$80,000.00	in	18 years
$160,000.00	in	24 years
$320,000.00	in	30 years
$640,000.00	in	36 years

If we are going to eradicate poverty, students must learn about capitalism and the stock market. Can you read the stock pages? What is the difference between a mutual fund and common stock? What is the difference between the net asset value and the offering price? What is a no-load fund? What are the Dow Jones, Nasdaq, and S&P?

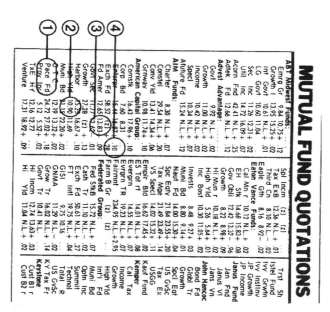

HOW TO READ A MUTUAL FUND COLUMN IN THE NEWSPAPER

1. The first column is the fund's abbreviated name. Several funds listed under a single heading indicate a family of funds.

2. The second column is the Net Assets Value (NAV) share at the close of the preceding business day. In some newspapers, the (NAV) is identified as the sell or the bid price — the amount (per share) you would receive if you sold your shares (less any deferred sales charges). Each mutual fund determines its net asset value of its shares outstanding. On any given day, you can determine the value of your holdings by multiplying the NAV by the number of shares you own.

3. The third column is the offering price, or, in some papers, the buy or the asked price. This is the price you would pay if you purchased shares. The buy price is the NAV plus sales charges. If there are no sales charges, an NL for no-load appears in this column, and buy price is the same as the NAV. To figure the sales charge percentage, divide the difference between the NAV and the offering price by the offering price. Here, for instance, the sales charge is 8.5 percent ($13.83 less $12.65 = $1.18; $1.81 divided by $13.83 = 0.085).

4. The fourth column shows the change, if any, in net assets value from the preceding quotation, in other words, the change over the most recent one-day trading period. This fund, for example, gained ten cents per share.

Economic Empowerment

Rather than take an exit exam that asks about Columbus and Shakespeare, can you imagine what would happen if every high school student was required to develop a business plan in order to graduate? Can you imagine what it would be like if every student, rather than taking a class in Eurocentricity, was required to take a class in entrepreneurship?

According to the research, boredom is the reason why our youth are dropping out of school in droves. They are bored with an irrelevant Eurocentric curriculum. We could reduce the dropout rate if we taught youth, especially African American youth and African American males, entrepreneurship. Since our youth are so into the bling bling and getting paid, let us help them by providing a mandatory class in entrepreneurship.

Ruby Payne should provide in-service training to teachers on entrepreneurship, which is one of the best ways to eradicate poverty—not to understand it, but to eliminate it.

Every school should provide their students with a monthly copy of the magazine *Black Enterprise*. Every student should receive a daily copy of the *Wall Street Journal*. Every student should be required to read Kevin Brown's book *From Welfare to Faring Well*. Kevin grew up in poverty, so he did not need to study it. He wanted to leave it. So he worked on his attitude and placed himself around positive people and was willing to volunteer to learn entrepreneurship. It is a fantastic story about a young man who grew up in poverty and now owns several McDonald's franchises. Kevin Brown is a multimillionaire.

Every student should read Farrah Gray's book *Reallionaire*. Farrah Gray also grew up poor. He didn't like it, didn't want to understand it, and didn't want to stay there. As early as seven years of age, he had a lemonade stand to earn income. He went on to develop several other businesses and has now become a millionaire with a best-selling book and a demanding speaking schedule. His desire is to become more than a millionaire, billionaire, or trillionaire. He calls himself a reallionaire.

Ruby Payne, we need to keep this thing real. We need to empower young people with an understanding of business principles, help them to find something that they like to do, some product they would like to make or sell, and let that be the springboard into starting a business.

Everyone, especially hopeful athletes, should read about the tremendous success of Magic Johnson. While many athletes retire broke or unable to maintain the standard of living they enjoyed while in professional sports, Magic Johnson is one of few athletes who literally is making more money off the court than he made while on.

Gale Sayers and Dave Bing are other successful athlete-entrepreneurs. Sayers was a brilliant running back for the Chicago Bears. He now owns a computer software company that grosses more than $40 million per year. Dave Bing, a superstar for the Detroit Pistons, is now a multimillionaire in the steel industry.

Ruby Payne, I would encourage you to review the great work of the Bill and Melinda Gates Foundation. Rather than understanding poverty, they decided they needed to eradicate it. The Gates Foundation created the Entrepreneurship High School in Cincinnati, which is the first of its kind. The school was started in 2002 and has already produced its first graduating class. It is a fantastic school, where the dropout rate is literally invisible because the students are excited about studying a relevant curriculum that can have immediate payoffs.

The Entrepreneurship High School does not have an attendance or truancy problem. Students have high GPAs and high self-esteem and confidence. They have been inspired to become MBAs and CPAs. This is how you address poverty. Ruby Payne, you should visit Dixon Elementary School in Chicago. Dixon also believes in teaching children entrepreneurship. A school store is managed and operated by the students, and an annual exhibit is provided for the larger community. Students show the products and services they have developed throughout the year. Can you imagine a school where the students understand income statements, balance sheets, cash flow statements, cost of goods sold statements, and are willing, ready, and able to tell you what all of that means?

I'm in favor of partnerships. Every business should adopt a school. Could you imagine if every student, in order to graduate, had to develop a business plan? The school's business partner could choose the top 10 business plans and provide financial packages. This would not only encourage and stimulate our youth, it would improve the economic climate in the Black community.

Every school should offer the program developed by the National Foundation for Teaching Entrepreneurship (NFTE). The founder, Steve Mariotti, and I are close friends and I am a consultant for NFTE. If Ruby Payne is sincere about poverty, she could learn a great deal from NFTE and Steve Mariotti.

In 1982, Steve made a momentous career change and became a special education/business teacher in New York City public schools. He chose to teach in such at-risk neighborhoods as Bedford-Stuyvesant in Brooklyn and the Ft. Apache section of the South Bronx. It was at Jane Adams Vocational High School in the Bronx that Mariotti had the idea to bring entrepreneurial education to low-income youth. This inspiration led to the founding of NFTE in 1987. Through entrepreneurship education, NFTE teaches young people ages 11 through 18 from low-income communities to become economically productive members of society by improving their academic, business, technology, and life skills. NFTE is now in every state in America and has trained more than 5,000 educators in the NFTE curriculum and has exposed that curriculum to hundreds of thousands of youth nationwide.

Eighty-three percent of NFTE students want to start their own businesses, compared with only 50 percent in traditional programs. Thirty-six percent of their students actually started a business of their own, versus 9 percent nationwide.

Seventy-six percent of NFTE students thought that starting and owning a small business was a realistic way out of poverty. Ninety-five percent indicated that NFTE gave them a positive view of business, and they were nearly twice as likely to predict that they would support themselves by owning a business.

NFTE's excellent textbook, *How to Start and Operate a Small Business,* includes the following chapters:

Chapter 1: What is Entrepreneurship?
Chapter 2: The Building Blocks of Business
Chapter 3: Return on Investment
Chapter 4: Opportunity Recognition
Chapter 5: Characteristics of a Successful Entrepreneur
Chapter 6: Supply and Demand
Chapter 7: Inventions and Product Development
Chapter 8: Selecting Your Business
Chapter 9: Cost of Running a Business
Chapter 10: What Is Marketing?
Chapter 11: Market Research
Chapter 12: Keeping Good Records
Chapter 13: Income Statement
Chapter 14: Financing Strategy

Economic Empowerment

Chapter 15: Negotiation
Chapter 16: From the Wholesaler to the Trade Fair
Chapter 17: Competitive Strategy
Chapter 18: Developing Your Market Mix
Chapter 19: Advertising and Publicity
Chapter 20: Break Even Analysis
Chapter 21: Principles of Successful Selling
Chapter 22: Customer Service
Chapter 23: Math Tips to Help You Sell and Negotiate
Chapter 24: Business Communication
Chapter 25: Sole Proprietorships and Partnerships
Chapter 26: Manufacturing
Chapter 27: The Production/Distribution Chain
Chapter 28: Quality
Chapter 29: Effective Leadership
Chapter 30: Technology
Chapter 31: Finding Sources of Capital
Chapter 32: Corporations
Chapter 33: Stocks
Chapter 34: Bonds
Chapter 35: The Balance Sheet
Chapter 36: Venture Capital
Chapter 37: Contracts
Chapter 38: Socially Responsible Business and Philan-
        thropy
Chapter 39: Small Business and Government
Chapter 40: Building Good Personal and Business Credit
Chapter 41: Cash Flow
Chapter 42: Protecting Intellectual Property
Chapter 43: Ethical Business Behavior
Chapter 44: Taxation and the Entrepreneur
Chapter 45: Insurance

Chapter 46: Franchising and Licensing
Chapter 47: International Opportunities
Chapter 48: Investment Goals and Risk Tolerance
Chapter 49: Investing for a Secure Future
Chapter 50: Exit Strategies

I've provided in-service training for teachers of NFTE and consulted on their textbooks. As you can see, they are serious about addressing the issue of poverty. NFTE does not want to "understand" poverty. They want to eradicate and eliminate it.

Operation Hope based in California is doing similar work. They have created the program Banking on Our Future, a national financial literacy program for youth ages 9-18.

Ruby Payne and her proponents should review these 50 chapters from *How to Start and Operate a Small Business.* That's how you address poverty. You teach young people entrepreneurship.

In my book *Hip Hop Street Curriculum,* we asked young people what they believed were the top three ways they could earn money in America. The three top answers were the NBA, rap, and drug dealing. Our youth do not believe that getting a good education is the best way to make it in America. They are well aware of the impact that racism has on their lives. They see unemployed or underemployed African American college students. Many young people will even challenge their teachers and ask them how much money they make! Then they will say, "I make that in a day selling drugs on the corner."

Our youth are aware that 50 Cent, P Diddy, Snoop, Russell Simmons, and numerous others are each worth more than $250 million. Let's review how young people view their economic options.

Economic Empowerment

NBA. Notice I didn't say sports, but NBA, which can either be the National Basketball Association or the National Black Association. More than 86 percent of the NBA basketball players are African American. You can count quickly the number of White Americans who play in the NBA. It is disappointing that 200 Black youth will try out for a basketball team but only one or two will try out for the debate or science fair teams. Many of our youth believe the only two sports are basketball and football. The following numbers tell the story.

1 million boys have a desire to make it into the NBA.
400,000 make high school teams.
4,000 make college teams.
35 are drafted into the NBA.
7 start.
4 years is the average career length in the NBA, 3 years in the NFL.

Can you imagine, there are a million young men, and now women, looking for seven full-time jobs that only last four years? I'm not trying to break the spirits of young people or take them away from their dream, but since there is a good chance they won't make it into the NBA, they need back up. Shaq, Michael Jordan, and Isaiah Thomas have college degrees.

Rap. Many African American youth do not believe it is important to master English because they're going to split infinitives all the way to the bank. Teachers try to convince me that our youth can't learn, yet these same youth can listen to a rap CD and literally—in five to ten minutes—memorize the words verbatim. That is a tremendous skill, and if only teachers understood that many students are auditory learners, they might provide fewer ditto sheets and left-brain lesson plans and more right-brain lesson plans. We will discuss this educational strategy in more detail in the last chapter. Listed below is the rap financial chart.

A rapper sells one million CDs at $18 for $18 million. Distributors receive 50 percent ($9 million). Producers receive 40 percent ($7.2 million). Rapper pays studio and video costs ($800,000). $1 million remains. IRS receives 50 percent. $500,000 remains. Rapper buys Lamborghini or Bentley. $0 remains.

I try not to discourage Black youth who desire to become rappers, but I do want them to see the economics of rap. Jay-Z and P Diddy are not only rappers. They are producers and entrepreneurs. They understand that the rap industry is a business and that you can sell a million CDs and broke if you don't understand the economics.

Drug Distribution. Why is it that if you have 499 grams of the original drug, cocaine, you receive a slap on the wrist and a homework assignment? If you have 5 grams of the derivative, crack cocaine, it's a mandatory jail sentence. If we have a war on drugs, why is it that 74 percent of all drug users are White but 70 percent of those convicted for possession are Black and Hispanic? Is there a war on drugs or a war on Blacks and Hispanics?

Do we really believe that we can incarcerate every brother who is in possession of 5 grams of crack cocaine and solve the drug problem? Almost 70 percent of inmates are in prison because of drug-related crimes. Europe understands this. They believe that the best strategy to address the drug issue is not through the penal system but through the medical system.

America spends $28,000 per inmate with a recidivism rate of 85 percent, while Europe spends $3,000 with a recidivism rate of 33 percent. You do the math.

Unfortunately, many of our youth believe they will be the first drug dealer who will never get caught. Ruby Payne, our youth understand poverty very well, and they believe that the best way to get out of poverty is to drop out of school and become a drug dealer. Listed below is a financial analysis of drug dealing.

$10,000 sales, best day
$700 average monthly net income
$8,400 yearly income
$84,000 maximum income over 10 years
Drug dealers do not retire. They either become addicts, felons, or die within 10 years.

We must expand our young people's horizons. We need to encourage them to think beyond the NBA, rap, and drug dealing. When I speak in youth assemblies, I ask them to give me a different career for each letter of the alphabet (including Q, X, Y, and Z). I don't let them use any sports or any entertainment careers.

If we want to eradicate poverty, we need to expand our young people's career range. Once a week, we should bring in a different professional who will inform them about their particular career. This is extremely important for African Americans because with the concentration of poverty in urban areas, they have never seen, talked to, or shook hands with an engineer, computer programmer, CPA, architect, etc.

We could reduce, eliminate, or eradicate poverty if schools improved their student-to-counselor ratio. In most inner city schools, the dropout rate hovers near 50 percent, and there is a ratio of 250 (even 500) students to 1 counselor. With figures like that, you can imagine the extent of the counseling taking place.

We need counselors who will expand students' career horizons, coordinate mentoring programs, help young people score high on the ACT and SAT before the last semester of their senior year, and remind them that Black colleges, while only possessing 16 percent of the Black students, produce more than 30 percent of the graduates. I'm concerned that White counselors will forget to tell African American youth about the efficacy of Black colleges.

If our young people can sell crack, they can sell CISCO. If they can sell rap CDs from the trunk of their cars, they can develop a business plan. If young people love hanging on corners and protecting their turf, they can master the principles of real estate. Can you imagine if Ruby Payne and her proponents came into a school and taught teachers and youth how to identify, purchase, rehab, and sell foreclosure properties in the neighborhood? A teacher could sponsor an after-school real estate club to conduct these activities in the real world, and the profit would be shared by the group. This would be so much better than telling teachers why they can't be effective with low-income students or how to understand poverty.

Could you imagine if Ruby Payne and her staff helped young people identify and buy a property in foreclosure for $5,000, and then rehabbed it for an additional $15,000, sold it for $100,000, and an $80,000 profit was equally distributed among the eight brothers who were involved in this endeavor?

Economic Empowerment

We could reduce the dropout rate dramatically. We could reduce and even begin to eradicate poverty.

Our youth are brilliant. I've seen young people without pencil, paper, or calculator convert kilos to grams and grams to dollar bills. Now these are the same students that the school labeled mathematically illiterate.

African American youth, males in particular, are prime candidates for understanding the stock market, entrepreneurship, and real estate. Donald Trump has nothing on young African American brothers. We need to teach our youth the principles of real estate. Remember, 1 percent of the population owns 57 percent of the wealth, and 10 percent owns 86 percent of the wealth. Do you think that Warren Buffett, who gave $37 billion to the Gates Foundation, earned that through the NBA, rap, or drug dealing? Or do you think that people like Bill Gates, Warren Buffett, Donald Trump, and the wealthiest 10 percent earn their money through entrepreneurship, the stock market, and real estate?

Ruby Payne, if you are serious about poverty and the achievement gap, should we not learn from this 10 percent how they acquired their wealth? Should we not teach African American and Hispanic youth how the 10 percent acquired their wealth? How many schools do you know of in America that offer classes in investment principles, entrepreneurship, and real estate?

In my book *Black Economics: Solutions for Economic and Community Empowerment,* I talk about entrepreneurship in detail. Unfortunately, because the African American community has been inundated with professionals who want to discuss poverty, it has not been taught the value and importance of entrepreneurship. The following example illustrates how significant this problem is in the Black community.

Entrepreneurs	Per 1,000
Arabs	107
Asians	96
Whites	60
Hispanics	17
African Americans	9

Numbers tell the story. Only nine African Americans per thousand start a business. Twenty-five percent of African Americans live below the poverty line along with 33 percent of African American children. Fifty percent of African American children live either at low-income level or below the poverty line. If we simply learned from other groups who seem to understand entrepreneurship, we could reduce poverty. There is an inverse relationship between entrepreneurship, Ruby Payne, and poverty. If we increase the former, we will decrease the latter.

Why do only nine African Americans per thousand start a business? Is it because their teachers are being counseled by Ruby Payne? Is it because schools are designed in Black communities to produce, at best, employees and not employers?

There is a different pedagogy and curriculum offered in AP, honors, and gifted and talented classes. Students are taught critical thinking skills and how to become employers. In fact, the entrance exam for some of these programs features only essay questions. The essay questions require students to use their reading and writing skills to critically think through the questions. Unfortunately, in regular, remedial reading, and special ed classes, students are taught to memorize lists and formulas.

Economic Empowerment

Another major reason why African Americans don't start businesses is the same reason why there are so many fights in our schools: self-hatred. African Americans fight each other because they hate themselves. The Willie Lynch letter shows us that as early as 1712, Africans were taught to hate each other by looking for differences among themselves.

The same thing applies to economics. African Americans are not poor. Last year they earned $723 billion. African Americans earn as much as Australians and Canadians. But because they hate themselves, they only spend 3 percent of their money with African American businesses. Ruby Payne, how can African Americans compete if White businesses receive 100 percent of revenue from White consumers and 97 percent from African Americans? This is economic violence.

How can African Americans win if they give 97 percent of their money to their competitors? Ruby Payne, we could reduce poverty in our community if your staff taught African Americans to spend a minimum of 10 percent of their money with each other.

When my late friend Harold Washington ran for mayor of Chicago, he observed that the 50 wards in the city had a $3 billion budget. Thirty-four wards were Black and Hispanic, and 16 wards were White. But for some strange reason, the 16 White wards were receiving $2 billion of the $3 billion budget. Harold Washington, in the spirit of fairness, ran a campaign based on the concept that each ward should receive 1/50th of the $3 billion budget. For most people that seemed fair and acceptable, but the people in power realized that if Harold Washington won the election, they would lose $1 billion. Frederick Douglass said, "Power concedes nothing without a struggle." They made life miserable for Harold Washington. Some people believe it was that pressure that killed him.

I challenge Ruby Payne and her staff to encourage African American students and their teachers to spend 10 percent of their money with African American businesses. We're no longer talking about poverty. We're talking about power.

Ninety percent of public school students in large urban areas are African American and Hispanic. Imagine that the citywide school budget is $3 billion, but less than 10 percent of the budget goes to African American schools. Ruby Payne, I challenge you to say to a school district, "Because African Americans are 80 percent of the student body, we recommend that 80 percent of the paint, plumbing, and food contracts be allocated to African American businesses."

If we are serious about poverty, we need to address the problem at the root, which is racism and capitalism. How can we continue to run school systems with dropout rates hovering near 50 percent? And while the dropout rate continues to rise, everyone on the budget is paid. How is it that school systems refuse to change the way budget money is disbursed to African American vendors?

I encourage Ruby Payne and her staff to teach Claud Anderson's concept of vertical integration, as outlined in the excellent book, *Powernomics*. If Asians were the only ones that consumed Chinese food, Chinese restaurants would not be a lucrative industry. If Italians were the only ones who consumed pizza, pizza parlors would not be a prosperous industry. In what areas of the economy do African Americans have a competitive advantage? What skills, talents, and resources do African Americans have that can be leveraged into an industry where, as Claud Anderson teaches, we control from beginning to end, from the natural resources to manufacturing, distribution, and retailing?

Can you imagine the result if African Americans told the Chinese community that their restaurants would be allowed in

Economic Empowerment

Black neighborhoods only when soul food restaurants were allowed in theirs? For every Chinese food restaurant in a Black neighborhood there must be a soul food restaurant in a Chinese neighborhood. For every Black dollar spent in a Chinese restaurant there must be a Chinese dollar spent in a soul food restaurant. This is power economics.

What if we told the NBA that African Americans would no longer play until we had a greater percentage of team ownership and ancillary contracts? The same with the NFL?

I respect rappers for their business acumen. What if more rappers got together and told the four distributors that control the music industry—EMI, BMG, Universal, and Warner—that they were pulling out until the 50 percent distribution rate was reduced?

If African Americans are the only ones who purchase Black hair care products, then how can we allow other companies to control that industry? We could have reduced poverty if we had maintained Johnson and Soft Sheen hair care products. We could reduce poverty if African Americans were taught by Ruby Payne and her proponents to only buy Black hair care products with the African queen on the bottle, which is the label approved by the Association of African American Health and Beauty Aids Institute. This trade organization was originally made up of 21 companies but is now down to approximately 10 because of monopoly capitalism and larger White companies buying out companies like Johnson and Soft Sheen.

Ruby Payne and her staff should teach African American students to study how certain industries can be controlled from beginning to end. She has said that in impoverished communities, people value "we" over "I" and cooperation over competition. These are the positive values we'll need in order to take control.

Ruby Payne and her staff should study the Nguzo Saba and Maat. One of the most important principles of the Nguzo Saba is *ujamaa*. *Ujamaa* is the Swahili word for "cooperative economics." They should teach African American children how other communities implement *ujamaa*. African Americans assume that immigrants and other groups that invade the Black community receive low-interest loans from the government. The reality is that these groups understand *ujamaa*. Let me describe a typical *ujamaa* meeting.

Step 1. Everyone brings $100 to the meeting.

Step 2. Everyone brings a business plan to the meeting.

Step 3. All agree that whoever has the best plan will receive all the money.

Step 4. The winner receives approximately $20,000 from the people who attended the meeting.

Step 5. The winner promises that he will only do business with the people in this room.

Step 6. Everyone meets back next week or next month to do it again so that all who desire and can qualify to receive seed capital will receive it through *ujamaa*.

Why do you think it has been difficult for African Americans to implement *ujamaa*? How is it that other groups can implement *ujamaa* in Black neighborhoods, but we can't do it for ourselves? It goes back to self-hatred and the need for every student to study the Willie Lynch Letter.

Ruby Payne, you should give the Willie Lynch Letter to your teachers. I will provide a copy here so that we can further understand why 25 percent of African American adults and 33 percent of African American children live below the poverty line.

The Willie Lynch Letter

Gentlemen, I greet you here on the banks of the James River in the Year of Our Lord 1712. First, I shall thank you, the gentlemen of the colony of Virginia, for bringing me here. I am here to help you solve some of your problems with slaves.

Your invitation reached me on my modest plantation in the West Indies while experimenting with the newest and still oldest methods for control of slaves. Ancient Rome would envy us if my program is implemented. As our boat sails south on the James River named for the illustrious King James whose Bible we cherish, I find enough to know that your problem is not unique.

While Rome used cords of wood as crosses for standing human bodies along the old highways in great numbers, you are here using the tree and rope on occasion. I caught the whiff of a dead slave hanging from a tree a couple of miles back. You are not only losing valuable stock by hangings, you are having uprisings. Slaves are running away. Your crops are sometimes left in the field too long for maximum profit. You suffer occasional fires. Your animals are killed.

Gentlemen, you know what your problems are. I do not need to elaborate. I am here to provide a method of controlling your black slaves. I guarantee every one of you that installed correctly it will control the slave for at least 300 years. My method is simple. Any member of your family or any overseer can use it.

I have outlined a number of differences among the slaves and I take these differences and make them bigger. I use fear, mistrust, and envy for control purposes. These methods have worked on my modest plantation in the West Indies and they will work throughout the South.

Take this simple little list of differences and think about them. On the top of my list is age, but it is there only because it starts with the letter A. The second is color or shade. There is intelligence, size, sex, size of plantation, attitude of owners, whether the slave lived in the valley, on the hill, east, west, north, south, has fine or coarse hair or is tall or short.

Now that you have a list of differences, I shall give you an outline of action. But before that I shall assure you that distrust is stronger than trust and envy is stronger than adulation, respect, or admiration. The black slave, after receiving this indoctrination, shall carry on and become self-re-fueling and self-generating for hundreds of years, maybe thousands. Don't forget, you must pitch the old black versus the young black male and the young black male against the old black male. You must use the dark skinned slaves versus the light skinned slaves and the light skinned slaves versus the dark skinned slaves. You must use the female versus the male and the male versus the female. You must also have your servants and overseers distrust all blacks, but it is necessary that your slaves trust and depend on us. They must love, respect, and trust only us.

Gentlemen, these kits are your keys to control. Use them. Have your wives and children use

68

them. Never miss an opportunity. My plan is guaranteed, and the good thing about this plan is that if used intensely for one year, the slaves themselves will remain perpetually distrustful.

Earlier I mentioned that all students should receive a monthly issue of *Black Enterprise*. In each issue of the magazine is a declaration of financial empowerment that reads as follows:

From this day forward I declare my vigilant and lifelong commitment to financial empowerment. I pledge the following:
To use home ownership to build wealth.
To save and invest 10 to 15 percent of my after-tax income.
To commit to a program of retirement planning and investment.
To engage in sound budget, credit, and tax management practices.
To measure my personal wealth by net worth, not income.
To be proactive and knowledgeable about investing, money management, and consumer issues.
To provide access to programs that will educate my children about business and finance.
To support the creation and growth of profitable, competitive, Black-owned enterprises.
To use a portion of my wealth to strengthen my community.
To ensure that my wealth is passed on to future generations.[11]

In your workshops for staff and students, Ruby Payne, you should provide a copy of the Declaration of Financial Empowerment from *Black Enterprise*. If you are serious about poverty, this is the way you eradicate it.

In the previous chapter, we looked at the major reason why there is an 88 percent differential between Black wealth and White wealth. The solution to this problem is not a Ruby Payne workshop on poverty. African Americans are not lazy. It is because of racism and capitalism.

Ten percent of the population owns 86 percent of the wealth through "old money." For some White families, generations of accumulated wealth began when they did not pay their African laborers from 1620 to 1865. They received hundreds of acres of free land thanks to the Homestead Act, and some got rich from the gold rush. They eliminated competition from Blacks in places like Tulsa, Oklahoma. And the list continues.

Ruby Payne and her staff should promote reparations if they are sincere about eradicating poverty. Listed below is a chart describing the historical precedent for reparations.

EXAMPLES OF REPARATIONS PAYMENTS

1952 Germany	$822 million	Holocaust Survivors
1971 United States	$1 billion + 44 million acres of land	Alaska Natives Land Settlement
1980 United States	$81 million	Klamaths of Oregon
1985 United States	$105 million	Lakota of South Dakota
1985 United States	$12.3 million	Seminoles of Florida
1985 United States	$31 million	Chippewas of Wisconsin
1986 United States	$32 million for 1836 treaty violations	Ottawas of Michigan
1988 Canada	$230 million	Japanese Canadians
1988 Canada	250,000 square miles of land	Eskimos and Indigenous People
1990 Austria	$25 million	Jewish Claims on Austria
1990 United States	$1.2 billion	Japanese Americans[12]

70

Economic Empowerment

America has compensated Asians who were placed in internment camps in California during World War II. America has provided reparations for land stolen from Native Americans. Why is it that America does not want to even discuss reparations to African Americans?

Ruby Payne and her staff should read the legislation that John Conyers, the congressman from Detroit, has placed before the Congress every year since 1969. The draft has yet to leave committee. Just like the teacher who said she doesn't see color, most White Americans are in denial.

A great math problem for students would be to calculate how much in reparations is due the African American community. Using the accounting principles of the IRS, students would factor in the cost of labor from 1620 to 1865 plus penalties and interest. Ruby Payne and her staff should calculate this figure. I wonder what it would be.

Lastly, Ruby Payne, I suggest you read the excellent book by Gary MacDougal, *Make a Difference: A Spectacular Breakthrough in the Fight Against Poverty.* MacDougal provides tremendous insight in his book. He points out that some states have been more effective than others in reducing poverty. For example, in 1996 in Illinois, 643,000 people were receiving assistance. In 2003, only 93,000 were receiving assistance, an 86 percent reduction. In contrast, in 1996, there were 143,000 people in Indiana receiving assistance. In 2003, 140,000 were still receiving assistance, only a 2 percent decline.

Ruby Payne, what did these two states do differently to achieve such drastically different results? According to Gary MacDougal, Illinois understood the importance of childcare. You don't take away a mother's welfare check and make her go to work yet perpetuate her responsibility for childcare. To put this in perspective, the average cost of day care for a child under two in Illinois is $34 per day. This adds up to $170 per 5-day workweek, which is 83 percent of what someone would earn working for the minimum wage. You either need to increase the minimum wage, or the state must provide a subsidy for childcare. Illinois has done that and as a result, has seen an 86 percent reduction in welfare recipients.

The same applies to transportation. If African Americans are not permitted to live in the section of town where the jobs are because of expensive housing, redlining, and racism, they will have to figure out a way to get to the jobs. But if there is no transportation system, as is the case in many suburbs, then how will they get there?

The state of Illinois partnered with various transportation companies to provide transportation for low-income residents to get to their jobs in affluent suburban communities. That's how you eradicate poverty.

One of the major reasons why inmate recidivism is 85 percent is that many felons who have been released from jail have had difficulty having their criminal records expunged or finding employers willing to hire them. The Safer Foundation in Illinois has considerable experience in ex-offender employment. They give employers the confidence to participate in the program. Safer works with both men and women ex-offenders on employment strategies. They also work with employers to provide jobs for participants. Ruby Payne and her staff should read about the Safer Foundation and their success in finding employment for ex-felons.

In the next chapter, we will look at the great work of Jonathan Kozol and his concerns about the economic injustice of school funding.

CHAPTER 5: SCHOOL FUNDING

Let's take a visit to a school in India. There is very little grass around the school, and the one tree near the school is almost dead. There is a small playground adjacent to the school, but it is also used as a staff parking lot. There is one bent basketball hoop, and there is broken glass on the playground.

The school building was built almost 100 years ago. The paint is chipping on the inside of the building, and it's a dark gray. The roof leaks, and on heavy rain days, students have to leave certain classrooms because there aren't enough buckets to catch the rain. When the students arrive in school, they are greeted by the principal with the angry sound of a blown horn, directing them to their classrooms. The students and their possessions must go through a metal detector.

Today is going to be a challenging day because it is cool this morning, in the low 40s, but the temperature is expected to rise to around 80 degrees. The janitor informs the principal that the antiquated heating and air conditioning system won't be working anytime soon. The principal and janitor decide that it will be best to use neither. So unfortunately, it will be a little cold for the children in the morning and possibly hot in the afternoon.

There are 34 students in the class, and everyone sits at a stationary desk. This is a sixth grade science class, which is being taught by an arts teacher because the full-time science teacher went on maternity leave in early September and will not be back until the next school year. Students receive physical education once a week, but unfortunately, they are unable to have band classes because there are no music teachers or instruments.

The children eat in their classrooms because the cafeteria is under construction. The lunch is delivered in a cold box. The teacher provides the lesson on the chalkboard, and lessons for the remainder of the day are also on the board. This is a typical experience in India.

Let's now travel to London, where the school is surrounded by a beautiful lawn, plentiful flowers, and thriving trees. There is a large playground where students can play soccer, basketball, cricket, hopscotch, and even engage in track events. The school was built seven years ago and has bright orange colors on the inside. The floor is always shiny. The children are greeted with a smile and are encouraged by the principal to have a good day.

It is expected to be cool in the morning, near 40 degrees, and rising to 80 in the late afternoon. The heat is on during the morning, but the air conditioning may be turned on later in the afternoon.

There are 17 students in the sixth grade math class. Students sit at computer terminals, and the teacher e-mails them the lesson for the day. The teacher has a master's degree in science. After the children review their e-mail, he delivers the lesson using a PowerPoint presentation. The students have a lab in their classroom. Later in the day, they will have band class, which is provided three days a week. P.E. is daily. At lunchtime, the students will go to the cafeteria for a nice, hot meal. The dining area accommodates 500 students.

Did I just describe India and London? I'm sorry. I meant to say an inner city school in Indianapolis, not India, and a suburb outside of Los Angeles, not London.

Jonathan Kozol has written two excellent books, *Savage Inequalities: Children in America's Schools* and *The*

Shame of the Nation: The Restoration of Apartheid Schooling in America. The titles alone describe the stark contrast between my two stories.

Let me now provide the quantitative data to support what you just read.

School District	Spending Per Pupil	% Student Population by Race		% Low Income
		B+H	White	
Manhasset, NY	$25,311	9	91	5
New York City	$12,627	72	28	83
Lower Merion, PA	$20,261	9	91	4
Philadelphia	$10,299	79	21	71
Highland Park (Chicago area)	$20,291	10	90	8
Chicago	$9,482	87	13	85

*B+H indicates Black and Hispanic.

State	Per-Student Funding in the Lowest-Poverty Districts	Per-Student Funding in the Highest-Poverty Districts	Gap Between Revenues Available per student in the highest- and lowest-poverty districts
Alabama	$6,646	$5,482	-$1,164
Alaska	$5,800	$7,422	$1,622
Arizona	$5,881	$5,243	-$638
Arkansas	$6,050	$5,695	-$356
California	$6,522	$5,988	-$534
Colorado	$7,093	$6,602	-$491
Connecticut	$9,083	$8,207	-$876
Delaware	$8,660	$8,672	$12
Florida	$6,375	$5,884	-$490
Georgia	$8,042	$7,418	-$624
Hawaii	*	*	*
Idaho	$5,998	$5,797	-$201
Illinois	$8,158	$5,613	-$2,545
Indiana	$6,791	$6,856	$64
Iowa	$8,355	$7,931	-$425
Kansas	$7,678	$7,169	-$510
Kentucky	$6,130	$5,917	-$212
Louisiana	$6,450	$5,458	-$992
Maine	$8,508	$7,994	-$514
Maryland	$8,033	$7,221	-$812
Massachusetts	$7,946	$8,416	$471
Michigan	$8,189	$6,884	-$1,305
Minnesota	$8,042	$8,703	$660
Mississippi	$5,475	$5,038	-$437
Missouri	$6,875	$6,398	-$477
Montana	$7,272	$6,070	-$1,202
Nebraska	$7,529	$7,448	-$81
Nevada	$6,220	$6,428	$208
New Hampshire	$8,192	$7,151	-$1,041
New Jersey	$10,221	$10,654	$433
New Mexico	$5,797	$5,915	$119
New York	$10,543	$7,613	-$2,930
North Carolina	$6,475	$5,899	-$577
North Dakota	$6,969	$6,968	-$1
Ohio	$8,080	$7,592	-$487
Oklahoma	$5,351	$5,109	-$241
Oregon	$6,357	$6,078	-$279
Pennsylvania	$8,618	$7,348	-$1,270
Rhode Island	$7,569	$6,873	-$696
South Carolina	$6,754	$6,779	$25
South Dakota	$6,671	$6,466	-$204
Tennessee	$5,258	$5,492	$234
Texas	$7,395	$6,190	-$1,205
Utah	$5,044	$5,499	$455
Vermont	$11,877	$10,970	-$908
Virginia	$7,860	$6,690	-$1,170
Washington	$6,672	$6,335	-$338
West Virginia	$7,122	$6,740	-$382
Wisconsin	$8,766	$8,245	-$521
Wyoming	$10,764	$9,370	-$1,394
USA	**$7,979**	**$6,542**	**-$1,436**

U.S. Department of Education

76

The conservative political activist in California, Ward Connelly, believes that there is a level playing field in America. He says that we do not need affirmative action. Ruby Payne says we need to understand poverty and its implications for children and their learning styles. She wants to help low-income children understand and appreciate middle-class values.

But what about my above tale of two schools, Ward Connelly and Ruby Payne? Is the problem low-income families or poorly funded schools? Why is there such a wide disparity in funding? Is there truly a level playing field in American schools?

We naively expect a child whose education costs only $12,627 to equally compete against a student whose education is funded at $25,311. Ward Connelly, this looks like affirmative action to me—for the benefit of the wealthy child. This is not a level playing field, and a workshop for teachers on how to teach low-income children middle-class values will not solve the problem. You don't need a Ph.D. in physics to realize that the answer to this problem is equal funding for schools. That may help address the root problem.

In the dedication, I mentioned Jesse Jackson and the great work he did for Harper High School in Chicago. Harper's pool was used to store old books rather than water. There were no band classes or musical instruments. The gymnasium was poorly lit. However, magnet schools in Chicago had everything students needed for a quality educational experience. This was not fair. Jesse Jackson is concerned about the disparity of funding throughout the state of Illinois as well as the entire country. This disparity in school funding transcends school districts and race.

This disparity of funding cannot be totally resolved by the governor. In some cities, magnet schools are used to appease the 5 to 15 percent White "majority" (even when they're in the minority). How can the 85 percent Black and Hispanic population in a school district be called the minority and the 15 percent White population be called the majority? The roots of racism are deep in this country.

Magnet schools, even under the leadership of a Black superintendent and/or a Black mayor, are often used to keep the 5 to 15 percent White population, as well as the Black middle class, from fleeing to the suburbs. Naively, African Americans often think that once one of "them" secures office, fundamental changes will take place in their lives. This is not always the case.

My book *Black Students, Middle-Class Teachers* documents that while race is still a factor, class is equally significant. The million-dollar question is, who's going to save poor African American youth?

More than 40 percent of teachers who have school-age children send them to private or magnet schools. Who knows the school better than the people who work there? Look at what they think of their own product.

What does Ruby Payne have to say about the disparity between magnet schools and poor schools? What does she say about the savage inequality of using property taxes to fund schools? Is that the best way to fund schools? I thought the state was the great equalizer. From a statewide perspective, is it fair for one school district to receive $25,311 while another district only receives $12,627?

I admire my friend Pastor James Meeks, who said that this funding disparity is unacceptable. He believes the governor should use whatever monies are available—income tax, sales tax, tax on vices, the lottery, the tollway—to close the gap. He told the governor of Illinois that if changes were not made, he would run for office, which would have thrown the Democratic Party in Chicago into complete chaos. Needless to say, a deal to level the playing field was struck on behalf of underserved students in Chicago's inner city.

What are Ruby Payne's strategies to correct the funding disparity? Will poverty workshops for teachers help poor Black children act middle class?

Quality Teaching

The Education Trust documents that there is a savage inequality in how schools are staffed. Ruby Payne and her proponents should read the Education Trust's report "Teaching Inequality: How Poor and Minority Students are Shortchanged on Teacher Quality." Poor minority children are all too often handicapped by incompetent, untrained, even uncertified teachers.

Despite clear evidence that brand new teachers are not as effective as they will eventually become, students in high-poverty and high-minority schools are disproportionately assigned teachers who are new to the profession. Children in the highest-poverty schools are assigned novice teachers almost twice as often as children in low-poverty schools. Similarly, students in high-minority schools are assigned novice teachers at twice the rate of students in schools without many minority students.

Students in high-poverty and high-minority schools are also shortchanged when it comes to employing teachers with a strong background in the subjects they are teaching. Classes in high-poverty and high-minority secondary schools are more likely to be taught by "out of field" teachers, those without a major or minor in the subjects they teach.

The situation in grades five through eight is even worse. In high-poverty and high-minority middle schools, about 70 percent of math classes, seven out of every ten classes, are taught by teachers who did not even have a college minor in math or a math-related field.

Teachers in the highest-poverty schools and highest-minority schools in a district were more likely to have failed the test of basic skills than teachers in the schools serving poor or minority students. In the highest-poverty schools in a district, one in eight teachers had failed the exam at least once, twice the rate of teachers in low-poverty schools. It is amazing to me how teachers love hearing Ruby Payne talk about bad, poor Black and Hispanic students but not about the rampant incompetence among faculty in poor and minority schools. I guess that's getting too close to home.

It's obvious that teachers prefer to blame the victims rather than look in the mirror to determine what they must do to improve or correct the problem. Researchers consistently have found that a teacher's competence in literacy, as measured by vocabulary skills and other standardized assessments, is related to student achievement. For example, in a study of teachers in several metropolitan Alabama districts, they found that a significant increase in the test scores of teachers who teach African American children would produce a substantial decline in the Black-White test score gap in that state.

William Sanders, who founded the Value Added Research and Assessment Center at the University of Tennessee, Knoxville, found that on average, low achieving students gained about 14 points each year on the Tennessee state test when taught by the least effective teachers, but more than 53 points when taught by the most effective teachers. In the last chapter on educational solutions, I will elaborate more on the great research of William Sanders, the Education Trust, and the Teacher Expectation Student Achievement (TESA).

Ruby Payne, what is your position on art teachers teaching math? What is your position on uncertified teachers teaching at all? What is your position on incompetent teachers who have been transferred from one low-achieving school to another, who have been protected by unions and due process, all to the detriment of students in low-income areas?

In *The Shame of a Nation,* Jonathan Kozol documents that the gross disparity in teacher salaries between the city and its affluent White suburbs have remained persistent. The median salary for teachers in New York City recently was $43,000, as compared to $81,000 in Manhasset. It should be obvious why inner city areas have a real challenge acquiring and keeping the best teachers. If there are greater challenges in the inner city, we must pay teachers in the inner cities more.

Ruby Payne, we don't need to provide workshops for teachers on how to better understand culturally deprived, low-income students. What we need to do is pay competent teachers more competitive salaries in the inner city.

One of the reasons why it has been so difficult to correct the funding disparity is the issue of state's rights. Within the 50 states, there are 3,067 counties, 95,000 public schools, and 15,000 locally controlled school districts in which 50 million children go to separate and unequal public schools. The only way to correct this problem is from a national and constitutional perspective. Ruby Payne, what is your position on the fact that 3,067 counties and 15,000 school districts are dictating policy on how schools are funded?

Presently, local school districts are determining the policy for the nation. In *Savage Inequalities,* Jonathan Kozol describes the stark contrast between East St. Louis, Illinois, and affluent suburbs across the bridge, surrounding St. Louis, Missouri.

> The chemical plants do not pay taxes in the East St. Louis area. They have created small incorporated towns, which are self-governed and exempt, therefore, from supervision by health agencies in East St. Louis. Aluminum Oil created a separate town called Allerton. Monsanto, Cerro Copper, and Big River Zinc are all in Sauget. National Stockyard has its own incorporated town as well. Basically, there's no one living in some of these so-called towns. Allerton is a sizable town. Sauget, on the other hand, isn't much more than a legal fiction. It provides tax shelters and immunity from authorities in East St. Louis. The town of Sauget claims a population of about 200 people. The town is named after the mayor. Monsanto uses East St. Louis as a dumping ground and has destroyed the water and the air, creating a myriad of health problems for African American children.[13]

Disparity in funding begins early. It does not begin on the first day of kindergarten. Kozol says that in New York City, for example,

Affluent parents pay surprisingly large sums of money to enroll their youngsters in extraordinarily early education programs, typically beginning at the age of two or three, to give them social competence and rudimentary pedagogic skills unknown to children of the same age in the city's poor neighborhoods. The most exclusive of the private preschools in New York, which are known to those who can afford them as "baby ivy," cost as much as $22,000 for a full day program. Competition for admission to these pre-K schools is so intense that private counselors are frequently retained at fees as high as $300 an hour to guide the parents through the application process.[14]

In *Class and Schools,* Richard Rothstein offers the following insight:

Fifty percent or more of minority and low-income children have vision problems that interfere with their academic work. A few require glasses, but more need eye exercise therapy to correct focusing, converging, and tracking problems. Some studies find that test scores of lower-class children who get therapy and free glasses rise relative to those children whose vision does not need support. In one experiment where therapy or lenses were provided to randomly selected fourth graders from low-income families, children who received optometrical services gained in reading achievement beyond the normal growth for their age while children in the control group who did not get these services fell farther behind.[15]

Ruby Payne, do we need workshops for teachers to better understand the learning styles and behavioral differences of low-income children, or do we simply need to provide them, in many cases, with glasses and eye therapy?

Is it too much to ask that low-income children receive full-day kindergarten, a safe school environment, eye therapy, and teachers who have passed the certification exam and are qualified to teach the desired subject? Is that too much to ask?

I want to create a virtual panel discussion with Ruby Payne, Jonathan Kozol, and Walter Williams. Throughout this book I have provided the reader with some of the positions of Ruby Payne. In this chapter, I've begun to share some of the concerns of Jonathan Kozol. Kozol believes that the major reason for the underachievement of African American students is because schools are not adequately funded.

Walter Williams, a professor of economics at George Mason University and a nationally syndicated columnist, wrote an article for the Washington Times. He said,

Teachers and politicians respond to the tragic state of affairs by saying more money is needed. The Washington, DC, school budget is about the nation's highest, with about $15,000 per pupil. The student-teacher ratio at 15 to one is lower than the nation's average. Despite this, Black academic achievement in DC is the lowest in the nation. Racial discrimination has nothing to do with the educational meltdown within the Black community. Where Black education is the very worst, often the city mayor is Black, the city council is Black dominated, and often the superintendent is Black, as well as most of the principals and teachers, and Democrats have run the cities for decades.[16]

With that opening statement, let us begin the panel discussion. Ruby Payne says the best way to close the gap is to understand the learning styles and values of low-income children and help them to develop middle-class values. She believes that teachers need to understand the cultural deprivation of low-income students.

Jonathan Kozol says that we must close the funding gap between the inner city and the affluent suburban school districts.

Walter Williams says that in DC, school funding, the students per teacher ratio, and middle-class African American leadership have not been enough to close the gap. I also want to add that ineffective districts can allocate $15,000 per child, but the million-dollar question is how much directly goes to the student and how much is siphoned off by the central office?

Most of my analyses and recommendations will be in the last chapter on educational solutions, but I want to ask here, how is it that Howard University has a greater graduation rate of African Americans than Harvard University? Harvard has more money, but Howard has a higher Black graduation rate. America does not like to talk about Cuba in a positive light, but how do we explain that country's 90 percent literacy rate while First World America struggles to reach 70 percent, and achieves far less among some populations.

Jonathan Kozol, I don't believe that we should measure schools based on dollars. Black college research refutes that

85

notion. Black colleges only have 16 percent of African American college students but produce 30 percent of African American graduates. You don't measure a school based on dollars. You measure a school based on who is in front of the class. If you force me to choose between an affluent school that Malcolm Little attended in Omaha, Nebraska, conducted by that racist, insensitive teacher, or a one-room school shack with Marva Collins as the teacher, give me Marva without a doubt or a question.

I am sensitive to Ruby Payne's concerns about poverty in Black America and the increasing number of low-income children attending our schools. I am even more sensitive to Jonathan Kozol's concerns about the disparity in school funding. You have to play the hand you're dealt. America's lack of will at the national, state, and local levels to equalize how schools are funded is the real problem.

Ruby Payne, you will not empower teachers by teaching them the cultural deprivation deficit model. In the last chapter, we will look at poorly funded schools in low-income areas that have been successful with African American students. According to a report by the Citizen's Commission on Civil Rights, a Washington, DC-based watchdog group,

Only 1 percent of the more than three million children trapped in failing schools nationwide have taken advantage of their government mandated option to attend a better school. A major reason why only 1 percent has been able to take advantage of transferring their children from a failing school to a higher performing one is that in most urban areas there are very few of those schools that exist, but more importantly that have space for additional students to attend. If the president had used his leadership to advocate for transfers not only *within* school districts but *between* them, the transfer option would have had real meaning. And indeed, if earnestly enforced, it might have opened up the possibility for mightily expanded racial integration in suburban schools surrounding our core cities.[17]

In the next chapter we will look at Kozol's second concern, and that's integration. He firmly believes that the two major impediments that affect the racial academic achievement gap are school funding and increasing segregation in America. We will look at integration and its impact on educating African American youth, as well as the fallacy of "Leave No Child Behind," a program that has great potential but is poorly funded and enforced.

CHAPTER 6: INTEGRATION

Earlier I provided a chart that clearly shows the relationship between income and education. I had to honestly ask myself if I really wanted to write a book refuting what seems so obvious. Integration is another factor that seems obvious. Michael Holzman, an independent consultant for the Schott Foundation, writes the following:

The National Center for Education statistics show that nearly 300 American high schools that are near 90 percent or more Black lose on average half their Black boys between grades nine and twelve. On the other hand, schools that have smaller proportions of Black students lose a smaller percentage. The least segregated American high schools with significant African American enrollment lose approximately one-quarter of their Black male students from grades nine to twelve, while it is 50 percent for segregated schools.

The most segregated American schools are to be found in the South and in the North. In New York, for example, which enrolls more African American students than any other district, among the 11 high schools that were 90 percent or more Black, only one relatively small school had more than half its Black male students entered grade twelve. In the city's big high schools, it was twice as likely that a Black male student would be missing from his senior class than present, and three times as likely that he would not get a diploma.

If we look at it the other way around, there are 32 New York high schools where Black male students have a better than even chance of conventional progress from grades nine to twelve. Of those, all but two have fewer than 100 Black male students, or less than half African American. Two out of 32 New York City high schools where Black male students have a 50-50 chance of conventional progress from grades nine to twelve enrolled about 10,000 of the city's African American high school students. The others enrolled about 90,000 black students.

These data indicate that, in general, segregated schools do worse than integrated schools, and big schools do worse than smaller schools. Big, segregated schools do worst of all. To return to our original question, does segregation of children in public schools solely on the basis of race deprive the children of the minority group of equal opportunities? It does. Why then does the practice continue?[18]

Integration

Integration

Percentage of Black Students in 90% - 100 Minority Schools

New York	61%
Illinois	60%
Michigan	60%
Maryland	53%
New Jersey	49%
Pennsylvania	47%
Alabama	46%
Wisconsin	45%
Mississippi	45%
Louisiana	41%
Missouri	41%
Ohio	38%
California	38%
Texas	38%
Georgia	37%
Florida	32%
Connecticut	31%
Massachusetts	26%
Indiana	23%
Arkansas	23%

[19]

U.S. CENSUS

This chapter focuses on integration and its impact on the achievement level of African American children. How can we dispute the Schott Foundation's findings that the more segregated the school, the greater the chance that African Americans and African American males specifically will not graduate? This is a major concern of Jonathan Kozol, who states the following in *Shame of a Nation:*

In Chicago, 87 percent of public school enrollment is Black or Hispanic. Less than 10 percent were White. In Washington, DC, 94 percent of the children were Black or Hispanic. Less than 5 percent were White. In St. Louis, 82 percent of the student body was Black or Hispanic. In Philadelphia and Cleveland, 78 percent. In Los Angeles, 84 percent. In Detroit, 95 percent. In Baltimore, 88 percent. And in New York City, over 75 percent of the students were Black or Hispanic.[20]

Gary Orfield of the Civil Rights Project at Harvard University adds the following:

American public schools are now 12 years into the process of continuous resegregation. The desegregation, which increased continuously from the 1950s to the late 1980s has now receded to levels not seen in three decades. During the 1990s, the proportion of Black students in majority White schools has decreased to a level lower than any year since 1968. Almost three-fourths of Black and Latino students attend schools that are predominantly minority and more than two million, including more than a quarter of Black students in the Northeast and Northwest, attend schools which we call "apartheid schools," in which 99 to 100 percent of students are nonwhite.[21]

Sheryll Cashin, in the book *The Failures of Integration,* offers the following:

Black and Latino public school students are now more separated into racially identifiable schools than at any time in the past 30 years. Nowhere are the affects of this retreat more palpable than in the South. Court ordered desegregation of African American students in the late 1960s and 1970s resulted in the South becoming the region with the most integrated schools. By 1988, the South reached the high point of 43.5 percent of Black students attending majority White schools, up from a mere 1 percent in 1954. But by 2000, marking a 12-year and continuing process of resegregation, only 31 percent of Black students in the South attended majority White schools.

Demographers have developed certain indices of our separation. One of them, an index known as the dissimilarity, measures the degree to which a racial group would have to move to be evenly distributed throughout a region in proportions commensurate with the group's percentage of the total population in that region. Detroit, one of the most segregated cities in the United States, has a dissimilarity index of 85, meaning that 85 percent of

Blacks in the Detroit metropolitan area would have to move in order to be evenly distributed in that area. Chicago's index is 81. Newark is 80. The national dissimilarity index for separation of Black people from Whites is 65. Sixty-five percent of all Black people in the United States would have to move in order to be evenly distributed among Whites.[22]

The Schott Foundation reports that integration is significant for student achievement, yet Kozol, Cashin, and Orfield say that the country is becoming more segregated every year. How do African Americans achieve the Schott Foundation's objective? How do they satisfy the concerns of Kozol, Cashin, and Orfield as the country becomes more segregated? How do Whites feel about integration? In his book *Two Nations,* Andrew Hacker provides the following insight on the White mindset:

The vast majority, some 85 percent, of Whites state they would like an equal mixture of Black and White neighbors. Unfortunately, this degree of racial balance has virtually no chance of being realized. The reason very simply is that hardly any Whites will live in a neighborhood or community where half the residents are Black. Here we have no shortage of studies. By and large, this research agrees that White residents will stay and some new ones may move in if Black arrivals do not exceed **8 percent.** But once the Black proportion passes that point, Whites begin to leave the neighborhood and no new

ones will move in. What makes integration difficult if not impossible is that so few Whites will
accept even a racial composition reflecting the
overall national proportion of 12 percent for African Americans.[23]

Cashin reinforces Hacker with the following analysis:

Whites are less likely than Blacks to want to live in
diverse neighborhoods. Studies show that Whites
are willing to pay a 13 percent premium to live in
all White neighborhoods. Three Harvard economists have concluded that this willingness to pay
more to live in predominately White areas best
explains the persistence of segregated neighborhoods. Overwhelmingly, White areas are less af-
fordable to racial minorities who tend to have less
income and wealth to underwrite their housing
costs.[24]

It is hardly news that bussing is extremely unpopular
among White parents. A mere 22 percent favor it as a method
to achieve integrated schools, compared to 55 percent of Black
parents. The Public Agenda, in collaboration with the Public
Education Network, conducted a comprehensive national study
entitled "A Time to Move On: African American and White
Parents Set an Agenda for Public Schools":

Nevertheless integrated schools continue to be a
desirable goal for both African American and White

parents. Approximately eight in ten Black parents and White parents feel integrated schools can help improve race relations in America, and 97 percent of parents agree that our country is very diverse and kids need to learn to get along with people from different cultures and ethnic backgrounds. But half of Black and 72 percent of White parents say integrated schools make little difference in the education children receive. Three-quarters of Black parents and 77 percent of White parents say too often the schools work so hard to achieve integration that they end up neglecting their most important goal: teaching children.[25]

Ruby Payne and Jonathan Kozol, are you able to honestly ascertain how Whites feel about integration? People will often give lip service about integration, but actions speak far greater than words. It is one thing for Whites to say they hold dear some of the dreams of Dr. Martin Luther King, but the reality is that the White threshold for toleration of Blacks hovers around 8 percent.

While many studies say that 75 percent of White Americans favor integration, for some strange reason 75 percent of White communities are not integrated. African Americans have been unable to integrate into White America because of racism. The following are examples of discrimination from race testers.

Lisa Lincoln, a Japanese American woman, inquired about a two-bedroom apartment in the Lakeview neighborhood of New Orleans, Louisiana. Lakeview is a moderately wealthy neighborhood of framed cottages and brick ranch houses. According to the latest census, it is 94 percent White in a city that is 67 percent Black. Upon inquiring, Lincoln was told the apartment was available. When she showed up with her boyfriend, who is Black, they were told that someone had already placed a deposit on the place.

Being suspicious, they arranged for a White friend to inquire about the apartment, who, as they predicted, was told it was available. They contacted the local fair housing agency, which sent testers to look into the apartment. All of the Black testers were told that the apartment had been rented, while all of the White testers were told it was available.

They filed a lawsuit, which resulted in a jury verdict in their favor with punitive damages of $100,000.

A Black couple in Chicago learned by telephone of an apartment available in the city's wealthy Near North Side area, which is 93 percent White. When they arrived to inspect the apartment, they were told, falsely, that it had been rented. They complained to the leadership of Metropolitan Open Communities, which sent five testers to the eight-unit building. Only the Whites were told that the apartment was available. The owners of the building settled the lawsuit for $100,000.

I could go on and on with examples of racism and discrimination. Michael Holzman and Jonathan Kozol, while I appreciate your concern regarding integration and its negative impact on the academic achievement of African Americans, how can these students integrate into a society, into a neighborhood, where they are not welcome?

How do African Americans feel about integration? The split between the demands of the leaders of the civil rights establishment and the concerns of their purported constituents has widened throughout the last 30 years. A majority of the Black populace disapproved of forced school bussing, while 68 percent of Black leaders supported bussing. The NAACP found this out when they ousted their Bergen county branch president. His crime was that he questioned the NAACP's long held posture that school integration holds the key to educational advancement for Black children. The respected civil rights leader wrote a letter to the state board of education arguing that racial balance was not the most important factor in addressing educational inequities. The NAACP found in a study gauging public opinion on the subject of school integration that they have a major problem.

The survey, conducted by a highly regarded think tank, Public Agenda in collaboration with Public Education Network, found that by a margin of eight to one, African American parents want public schools to focus more on raising academic achievement standards than on promoting integration and diversity. According to one Black parent from Pennsylvania, "We spent a lot of time on race issues, and we need to redirect some of those energies to getting our children better educated."

Milwaukee has experienced something similar. The busing system implemented to ensure diverse school enrollment was complex and costly. The burden of busing students to cross-town schools was placed primarily on Black students. It was an issue of how do we least disrupt the White community. Placing the busing burden on Black students was not warmly received by all. Civic leaders who opposed busing thought the only thing it did was shift Black students across town to other Black schools. Eighty-five percent of all students bused in the Milwaukee area were Black. Black families soon grew tired to carrying the weight of integration and began expressing their discontent.

This was also felt in Evanston, Illinois, which has been a bastion for the will to secure integration. The district wants to keep its 60 percent guideline intact, which says that no school should ever have more than 60 percent either Black or White population. But parent activists in west central Evanston have lobbied the district to scrap its integration plan and build a new school in their neighborhood, charging that children there were bused excessively, hurting them academically. Among elementary school students in District 65, about nine of every ten Whites met or exceeded standards in reading and math, compared with about five of every ten African Americans in reading.[26]

More than 80 percent of American children are bused. White America is not against busing. It is against their children being bused for racial reasons, for integration, and they are not in favor of African American children being bused into their neighborhoods.

Nor are African Americans in favor of integration and busing if they are to bear it by themselves. Not only are their children spending two to four hours daily on buses without the promise of academic achievement, but the long distances that their children's schools may be away from their homes makes it difficult for parents to attend PTA meetings and other school activities.

An interesting twist on how to achieve balance, and I'm sure Ruby Payne would appreciate this, comes from North Carolina's Wake County public school system, a dynamic and growing district of more than 120,000 students that includes the city of Raleigh and its surrounding suburbs. The school board voted to replace a longstanding racial integration plan with a less racially focused goal, that no school should have more than 40 percent of its students eligible for free or reduced-price lunch, or have more than 25 percent of its students performing below grade level. Their rationale is that schools with high concentrations of poverty tend to offer a difficult environment for learning. According to a study conducted for the Economic

Policy Institute, low-income schools are 24 times less likely than middle-class schools to be consistently high performing.

In Wake County, educators observed that schools with high concentrations of poverty had high teacher turnover, low parental involvement, and high student mobility. Wake County decided to implement economic school integration by withdrawing school district boundaries and partly by making extensive use of magnet schools with special arts and music programs. Almost all of the specially themed magnets, which were established during the district's effort to promote racial integration, are located in high poverty areas in Raleigh. In general, 30 percent of the magnet school students are assigned from the local neighborhoods, and the rest are drawn in from other areas. If the integration policy is driven by income and not by race, this may be one way to appease some racists.

I can't dispute the research that Jonathan Kozol, Gary Orfield, and Matthew Holzman have provided, that segregated schools fare worse in furthering the academic achievement of African American students than highly integrated schools.

As I've mentioned, I'm not trying to sell poverty. I would love for all African American children to be in middle- to upper-income homes, where their fathers are present and working and their mothers, who stay at home, possess a master's degree. I would love for America to achieve Martin's dream of a beloved community where we are valued, not by the color of our skin, but by the content of our character.

Kozol, Orfield, and Holzman, African Americans cannot make White people accept them. Whites are willing to spend a premium to live in segregated communities. African Americans cannot live in neighborhoods where racism is rampant and the White threshold is only 8 percent. If, as you say, integration is key to improving the academic achievement of African American students, how do we deal with White resistance to this goal?

Integration

I support the increase of funding for African American students, but you have to play the hand you're dealt. In the next chapter, which I think is the most significant in the book, I'm going to play the hand that we've been dealt—that shows 25 percent of African American adults and 33 percent of our children living below the poverty line. That shows only 32 percent of our children having their fathers present in the home. That shows schools becoming more and more segregated each and every day. Yet, in spite of those issues, it is possible to successfully educate African American students.

Lastly Kozol, Orfield, and Holzman, from an Africentric perspective, there is a distinction between integration and desegregation. Integration is done between equals. There is mutual respect. All parties are considered and equally share in the integration process. What has taken place primarily in America is desegregation. An example is one-sided busing. The burden of desegregation has been placed mostly on the Black community. With true integration, the bus carries both Black and White passengers.

Not only should children be integrated, but staff as well. African American children are 17 percent of the student body, but their teachers are only 6 percent of the faculty. In schools where African American children are bused, the percentage is often less than 1 percent for the teachers.

True integration requires that changes be made to the curriculum. You can't say you have an integrated school if you have a Eurocentric curriculum. You can't say you have an integrated school system, and then earmark the shortest month of the year, February, for glancing at the contributions of African Americans. If a school is truly integrated, there will be a multicultural curriculum.

If a school is integrated, not desegregated, then the pedagogy will be integrated. Children learn in different ways. You can't say you have an integrated school when you primarily teach, using a left-brain pedagogy. If the children in your school are right-brain learners, you must integrate the pedagogy to account for right-brain learning styles. Right-brain lesson plans would include writing, oral reports, drawing, fine arts, and the use of artifacts in assignments and activities.

How many integrated schools in America have achieved mutual respect, equally shared busing, a racially balanced staff, a multicultural curriculum, and a whole-brain pedagogy?

I would like for Kozol, Orfield, and Holzman to acknowledge that schools can look integrated or desegregated on the outside but can be highly segregated on the inside. Thurgood Marshall, the brilliant lawyer who orchestrated the integration decision in Brown vs. Topeka in 1954, and many others underestimated entrenched racism and White supremacy in this society.

There are many desegregated schools, but if you look carefully at the classrooms, you will see new forms of segregation, which are called tracking and special education. A desegregated school could be 50 percent Black and 50 percent White on the outside, but the AP, honors, and gifted and talented classes reveal a less than equal playing field in educating African American and White students. Nationwide, only 3 percent of gifted and talented students are African American.

On the other end of the education spectrum, we have special education. African American students comprise 41 percent of the students placed in special education. The school could be integrated on the outside, but predominantly White in advanced placement, honors, and gifted and talented, slightly desegregated in the regular classes, and predominantly Black and Hispanic in remedial and special ed classes.

In the next chapter, we will provide educational solutions for low-income students in response to Ruby Payne's poverty theory.

CHAPTER 7: EDUCATIONAL SOLUTIONS

Reading skills on entering kindergarten by race and socioeconomic status

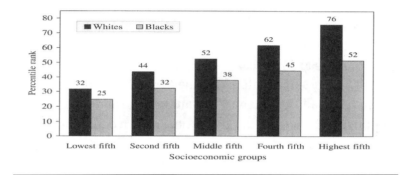

Mathematics skills on entering kindergarten by race and socioeconomic status

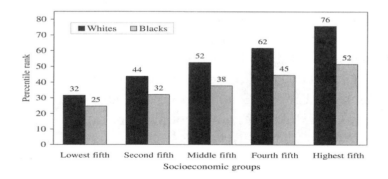

Segregated schools – African American male dropout rate: 50 percent.

Integrated schools – African American male dropout rate: 25 percent.

I want the reader to review the above significant charts. The first chart reinforces the Coleman study that correlates income and education. This is the major premise of Ruby Payne.

Kozol's chart illustrates the difficulties of educating children because of inadequate funding.

Holzman and the Schott Foundation document that the more segregated a school, the lower the academic achievement of African American students.

These are our challenges, and throughout this book I've attempted to address them. They are very formidable. I do not belittle the impact that family income has on educational outcomes. I do not discount the tremendous significance of one school district receiving $5,000 to $10,000 more per child than another school district. Nor do I belittle the significance of educating African American children in integrated environments. However, in spite of these three obstacles, there are schools, programs, and strategies that can overcome them. Let me begin with teacher quality.

My fundamental disagreement with Ruby Payne is that her teacher workshops should focus on teacher quality. In my workshops, I do not allow teachers, who control the experiences of children from 9:00 am to 3:00 pm, to talk about what parents in the home do or do not provide. Nor do I allow parents to talk about what teachers are or are not doing from 9:00 to 3:00.

Blaming others conveniently lets us off the hook. There is enough blame to go around in our public schools. Educators do not have the interest, ability, or expertise to resolve the economic problems that face African American families. If poverty is going to be the major focus, then educators should

Educational Solutions

be taught how to reduce, eliminate, or eradicate poverty. Teachers have enough challenges trying to properly teach reading and math, much less expecting them to reduce the income disparity of African Americans who only earn 64 percent of White income.

Importance of Quality Teaching

In this last chapter, I will focus on what educators can do, and I want to start with the excellent research of William Sanders and his document, "Good Teaching Matters."

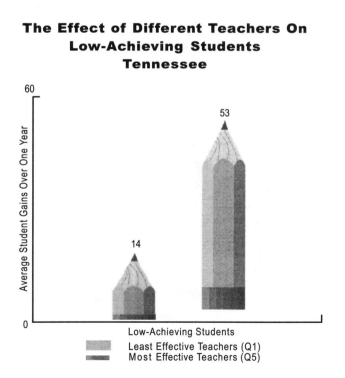

The Effect of Different Teachers On Low-Achieving Students Tennessee

Average Student Gains Over One Year

60

53

14

0

Low-Achieving Students
Least Effective Teachers (Q1)
Most Effective Teachers (Q5)

Sanders, William L. and Rivers, Joan C. "Cumulative And Residual Effects of Teachers on Future Student Academic Achievement."

105

Cumulative Effects of Teacher Sequence on
Fifth Grade Math Scores: Tennessee

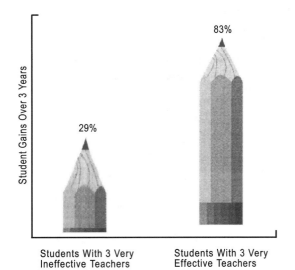

Sanders, William L. and Rivers, Joan C. "Cumulative And Residual Effects of Teachers on Future Student Academic Achievement."

Educational Solutions

Boston Students With Effective Teachers Showed Greater Gains

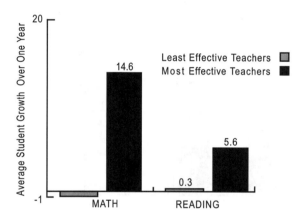

Source: Boston Public Schools, "High School Restructuring," March 9, 1998.

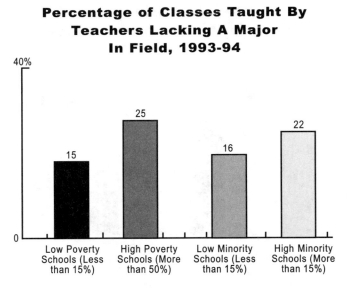

**Percentage of Classes Taught By
Teachers Lacking A Major
In Field, 1993-94**

Source: Richard Ingersoll, University of Georgia, Unpublished, 1998.

Educational Solutions

African American Students Are More Likely To Have Underqualified Teachers: Tennessee

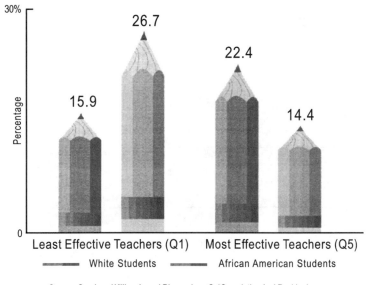

Source: Sanders, William L. and Rivers, Joan C. "Cumulative And Residual Effects of Teachers on Future Student Academic Achievement."

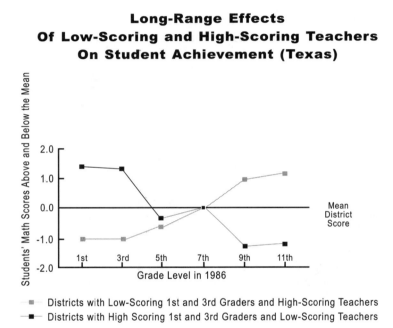

**Long-Range Effects
Of Low-Scoring and High-Scoring Teachers
On Student Achievement (Texas)**

Districts with Low-Scoring 1st and 3rd Graders and High-Scoring Teachers
Districts with High Scoring 1st and 3rd Graders and Low-Scoring Teachers

Source: Ronald F. Ferguson, "Evidence That Schools Can Narrow
the Black-White Test Score Gap," 1997.

110

Effects On Students' Reading
Scores In Dallas (Grades 4-6)

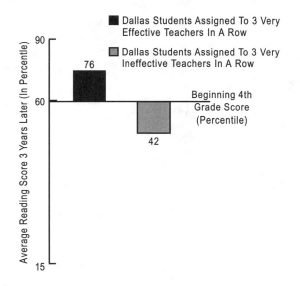

■ Dallas Students Assigned To 3 Very
Effective Teachers In A Row

▨ Dallas Students Assigned To 3 Very
Ineffective Teachers In A Row

Beginning 4th
Grade Score
(Percentile)

Average Reading Score 3 Years Later (In Percentile)

90

76

60

42

15

Source: Heather Jordan, Robert Mendro, & Dash Weerasinghe,
"Teacher Effects On Longitudinal Student Achievement" 1997.

111

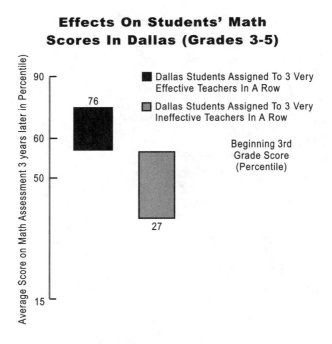

Effects On Students' Math
Scores In Dallas (Grades 3-5)

Average Score on Math Assessment 3 years later in Percentile)

90

76

60

50

27

15

■ Dallas Students Assigned To 3 Very
Effective Teachers In A Row

▨ Dallas Students Assigned To 3 Very
Ineffective Teachers In A Row

Beginning 3rd
Grade Score
(Percentile)

Source: Heather Jordan, Robert Mendro, & Dash Weerasinghe,
"Teacher Effects On Longitudinal Student Achievement" 1997.

112

Educational Solutions

Dr. Sanders has shown that students gain about 25 percentile points if they have three consecutive years of teachers who are in the top quintile of effectiveness (in my paradigm, teachers and coaches).

William Sanders' research has shown that *two consecutive years of an ineffective teacher could destroy a child for life*. Children are not yo yos. They don't have the resilience to withstand a bad first grade teacher, a good second grade teacher, a bad third grade teacher, etc. According to the Report on Teacher Quality by Education Trust, many African American and Hispanic children in low-income areas have experienced several years of ineffective teachers (custodians, referral agents, and instructors). Forty-four percent of students, primarily in low-income Black and Hispanic neighborhoods take at least one class with a teacher who did not major in math or science "attempting" to teach that subject. *Good teachers may cost more, but ineffective teachers cost the most.*

Ruby Payne, we could squash the poverty theory if we simply followed the research findings of William Sanders and ensured that our children received at least two to three consecutive years of effective teachers. Two to three consecutive years of effective teachers can overcome family poverty, inadequate school funding, and segregation.

William Sanders' findings are reinforced by research conducted by the University of Virginia study "Academic and Social Advantages for At Risk Students Placed in High Quality First Grade Classrooms." Classroom teachers who provide instructional and emotional support can improve academic outcomes for first graders who are considered at risk for school failure. The sample of 910 children is drawn from the National Institute of Child Health and Human Development's study of early childcare and youth development.

113

If placed in classrooms offering low instructional quality, children whose mothers had less than a four year college degree, scored lower than their peers on achievement tests. If placed in supportive classrooms when instruction was direct and children received regular feedback on their work, they performed as well as pupils with more highly educated mothers. Children who displayed social, behavioral, or academic problems in kindergarten could overcome those difficulties in first grade and perform as well as those without such problems if they were placed in classrooms with a teacher who displays warmth and sensitivity. If assigned to teachers who did not have those traits, they scored lower than their classmates on measures of achievement and adjustment.[27]

Good teaching matters. Good teaching can overcome income disparities, funding disparities, and segregation. This is why I am in favor of looping. While two consecutive years of an ineffective teacher can destroy a child for life, two consecutive years of an effective teacher can catapult a child into lifelong success.

- Teachers who see strengths in students teach positively.
- Teaching to students' strengths helps students see themselves positively.
- If students come to us from strong middle-income families, it makes our job easier.
- If they do not, it makes our job crucial.

Let's say there are two first grade classrooms, one taught by a master teacher or coach and one taught by a custodian, referral agent, or instructor. The principal implements looping for three years. When the effective teacher, who has the students from first through third grades, passes them to the fourth grade, they are reading at fifth, sixth, and seventh grade levels. The students in the classroom with the ineffective teacher are passed to fourth grade, but they are reading at a third to fourth grade level.

Ruby Payne, Kozol, Orfield, and Holzman, how do we explain the difference? The students are still poor. Their school is inadequately funded and 100 percent Black. Yet, there is a significant difference in their educational achievement. Good teaching matters.

Unfortunately, we had to lose the class of students who for two to three years were poorly educated by the custodian, referral agent, or instructor. But hopefully, after the two or three years, we will be able to fully document that it was never the children, their low-income parents, or the mothers who lacked a college degree. It was always the classroom teacher, Ruby Payne. I am only in favor of looping with custodians, referral agents, and instructors for research purposes. Ideally, we should only loop with master teachers because we cannot afford to lose students with two consecutive years of incompetence.

Ideally, custodians, referral agents, and instructors should be removed, but unfortunately, because of strong unions, they are able to remain. We must have our best teachers in the early grades. Principals tell me they place their best teachers in the higher grades because they're needed to maintain order. What a band-aid solution. That's like a sports team holding the best player until the last quarter to play. By then it's too late.

The best teachers need to teach in the primary grades. If I were a principal, my best teachers would not teach eighth grade but kindergarten. My best teachers would teach kindergarten and first grade, and my worst teachers would teach eighth grade. By the time the children reached eighth grade, they would be testing at the eleventh or twelfth grade level, and there would be nothing a custodian or referral agent could do to destroy them.

By the time my children reached eighth grade, I would have removed that incompetent teacher anyway. Because I'm an advocate of teacher quality, all of my teachers would be trained in Teacher Expectation Student Achievement (TESA). As you know, Ruby Payne, many teachers lower their expectations based on race, income, gender, and appearance. Rather than teachers discussing the tremendous impact that family income has on student outcomes, which teachers have no control over anyway, they should focus on their expectations. TESA documents a direct correlation between increased expectations and improved academic achievement.

The teachers who tell me they do not see color are the same teachers who say they believe that all children can learn and they have the same expectations for all their children. Fortunately, through TESA, we can now quantify expectations. For example, when teachers have high expectations of their students, there is an equitable distribution of response opportunities.

One way to achieve equitable distribution of response opportunities is to write the names of your children on index cards and place them in box. A. When you want to call on a student, pull a name out of the box. When the answer is given, place the card in box B. Continue to call on students from box A until all the names have been called and then repeat the process. There really is a science to being a master teacher.

TESA research documents that teachers that have high expectations give equal feedback to all students. You cannot say that you have high expectations for all students if you give more feedback to some students than others. Some teachers give more feedback to middle-class students than low-income students. Ruby Payne, the issue may not be the income of the parent but how teachers perceive income and how that affects their expectations.

It is unfair for a teacher to engage a middle-income student for four minutes until the child gives the correct answer, but the low-income child receives only 30 seconds of feedback. Ruby Payne, is the issue income or expectations? I believe it's expectations, and many teachers lower their expectations based on income.

There was an excellent article written almost a decade ago that is just as relevant today. In "The Pedagogy of Poverty vs. Good Teaching" Martin Haberman says, "Teaching acts that constitute the core function of urban teaching are giving information, asking questions, giving directions, making assignments, monitoring seat work, reviewing assignments, giving tests, reviewing tests, assigning homework, reviewing homework, settling disputes, punishing noncompliance, marking papers and giving grades."

The typical assignment as outlined in "The Pedagogy of Poverty" is, "take out your dictionaries and write the words that begin with H." This philosophy appeals to several constituencies:

1. It appeals to those who themselves did not do well in school. People who have been brutalized are usually not rich sources of compassion, and those who have failed or done poorly in school do not typically take personal responsibility for that failure. They generally find it easier to believe that they would have succeeded if only somebody would have forced them to learn.

2. It appeals to those who rely on common sense rather than thoughtful analysis. It is easy to criticize human

and developmental teaching aimed at educating a free people as mere permissiveness, and it is well known, they say, that permissiveness is the root cause of our nation's educational problem.

3. It appeals to those who fear minorities and the poor. Bigots typically become obsessed with need for control.

4. It appeals to those who have low expectations for minorities and the poor. People with limited vision frequently see value in limiting unfamiliar forms of pedagogy. They believe that at-risk students are served best by directive, controlling pedagogy.

Unfortunately, current teaching methods outlined in "The Pedagogy of Poverty" do not work. Youngsters achieve neither minimal levels of skill nor learn what they are capable of learning. The classroom atmosphere created by constant teacher direction and student compliance seethes with passive resentment that sometimes bubbles up into overt resistance. Teachers burn out because of the emotional and physical energy they must expend to maintain their authority every hour of every day. Teachers who began their careers as helpers, models, guides, stimulators, and caring sources of encouragement end up as directive authoritarians in order for them to function in urban schools.

The National Commission on Teaching recommends the following:

1. All children must be taught by teachers who have the knowledge, skills, and commitment to teach children well.

Educational Solutions

2. All teachers-education programs must meet professional standards or they will be closed.

3. All teachers must have access to high-quality professional development and regular time for collegial work and planning.

4. Both teachers and principals must be hired and retrained based on their ability to meet professional standards or practice.[28]

Teacher expectations, not family income, are the most important factor in determining educational achievement. We need to return to Rule 110. Before integration, Jonathan Kozol and Gary Orfield, Black teachers and strong White teachers required Rule 110. They were not in denial, and they told African American students that the country was racist. Holzman, this is the way you overcome segregation. You tell your students that the country is racist. You explain why there are certain people who do not want you to live in their neighborhoods. You tell them that if they want to make it in America, they will have to score more than 80, 90, or even 100. Tell them that they have to be the best. Later, when we discuss the great work of historically Black colleges and universities, we'll learn that Rule 110 and being honest about racism are the secrets to their high graduation success rates.

Unfortunately, there are many liberal teachers today who allow Black children to wear their caps in the building. They allow belts to be unbuckled, pants to sag, and shoes to be untied. Ruby Payne, now that Black youth have heard how important income is, they are now playing the victim. "Come on, teacher, give me a grade" or "I'm Black and fatherless." Many teachers think they're helping African Americans by

119

employing social promotions and grade inflation—but they're not. The U.S. Department of Education reports that seven percent of students from low-income families are socially promoted, whereas less than 2 percent of students from higher-income families.

As much as I'm an advocate of discipline—one of my books is titled *Developing Positive Self Images and Discipline in Black Children*—I am also in favor of retaining students. I'm very much aware of research findings that state that retaining students affects self-esteem and increases the risk of dropping out, but a student should not be reading at a fourth or fifth grade level in ninth grade.

I also agree with the statement, "If you keep doing what you've been doing and expect a different outcome, that borders on insanity." Therefore, if we're going to retain the student, it is senseless to deliver the student into the hands of another custodian, referral agent, or instructor who uses left-brain lesson plans with the emphasis on ditto sheets and a Eurocentric curriculum wherein Columbus still discovers America, Lincoln frees the slaves, and Egypt is moved from Africa to the Middle East.

If we are going to retain students, the burden of education should not just be borne by the students but also by the system. African American students should be guaranteed a master teacher, right-brain lesson plans, an Africentric curriculum, cooperative learning, a smaller student-teacher ratio, and single-gender classrooms. Any one of those components will improve academic achievement. The more that are utilized, the more effective we will be.

Let me share with you some very interesting scholarship that, ironically, comes from a White professor, Thomas Dee of Swarthmore College. His article is titled "Teacher's Race and Student Achievement in Randomized Experiment."

Educational Solutions

In brief the result of the test score evaluations indicate that exposure to an own race teacher did generate some substance of gain in student achievement for both Black and White students. More specifically these results suggest that a year with an own race teacher increased math and reading scores by 3-4 percentile points. Notably the estimated achievement gains associated with an own race teacher exist for nearly all groups of students defined by race, gender and several observed student, teacher and community characteristics. Overall, the results of this study provide evidence that ongoing efforts to recruit minority teachers are likely to be successful in generating improved outcomes for minority students.

The prior literature offers at least two general explanations why the racial pairing of students and teacher might exert an important influence on student achievement. These explanations are not mutually exclusive. One class of explanations involves what could be called passive teacher effect. These effects are triggered by the racial presence and not by explicit teacher behaviors. For example: one frequently cited reason for the relevance of a teacher's race is that by its mere presence the teacher's racial identity generates a sort of role model effect that engages student effort, confidence and enthusiasm. For example: it is possible for an underprivileged Black student in the presence of a Black teacher who encourages them to reach their full potential. Similarly, students may feel more comfortable and focused in the presence of an own race regardless of the teacher's behavior. An alternative class of explanation for the educational benefits of own race teachers, points to active teacher effects. Race specific patterns of behavior among teachers including allocating class time and interacting with students and designing class materials, may indicate that teachers are more oriented toward students that share racial or ethnic background. For example: prior studies have indicated that Black students with White teachers receive less attention, are praised less, and scolded more than White counterparts.[29]

The challenge to Thomas Dee's research on the significance of the racial background of the teacher, not family income, Ruby Payne, is that only 6 percent of America's teaching core is African American. According to Kozol, Orfield, and Holzman, since 1954 and integration, there has been a 66 percent decline in African American teachers. I strongly recommend every state implement South Carolina's Call Me Mister program. On most state campuses, they provide scholarships and mentoring to increase the paltry one percent of African American male teachers. I have been actively involved in their mentoring.

If we provided African American children, kindergarten through eighth grade, with nine master teachers who were African American, we would break all kinds of records. If we combined the concept of looping and same-race teachers and had an African American master teacher loop from kindergarten through eighth grade, we could refute the research of Payne, Kozol, Orfield, and Holzman.

Educational Solutions

As I've said, I've learned to play the hand I've been dealt. In my book *Black Students, Middle Class Teachers,* a White female teacher and a Black boy are shown on the cover to reinforce the idea that it is not the race or gender of the teacher that makes a difference but his or her expectations of students.

Let me share Thomas Dee's second finding. If you thought his findings on race were controversial and significant, you're going to love this theory. Thomas Dee documents that having a male teacher improves the performance of boys while harming girls' reading skills. On the other hand, a year with a female teacher would close the gender gap in science achievement among 13-year-old girls by half and eliminate the smaller achievement gap in mathematics.

Dee found that assigning boys to male teachers and girls to female teachers significantly improved the achievement of both boys and girls, as well as teacher perceptions of student performance and engagement with the teacher's subject. This is very interesting research on the significance of race and gender in education.

The challenge is that only 1 percent of teachers are African American males. It is possible for Black boys to go K-8 and never experience a Black male teacher. I would love for a superintendent to implement a single-gender school with single-gender master teachers. If that's too difficult to achieve, principals can create single-gender classrooms of boys with an African American male master teacher, and have that teacher loop the students from kindergarten through eighth grade. I would also like to see that take place for African American girls.

We could then retire Payne, Kozol, Orfield, and Holzman's theories.

I work with schools where there are few African American teachers and even fewer African American male teachers. As we've learned from TESA and William Sanders, it is not the race or the gender of the teacher but the expectations they have of their students. Let me be clear. A White female teacher, Thomas Dee, with higher expectations and better classroom management skills would be more effective than an African American female or male teacher with lower expectations and poor classroom management skills.

Eighty-three percent of elementary school teachers are White and female. I've had to reconcile the fact, from an Africentric perspective, that the future of the Black race lies in the hands of White female teachers.

I have also seen how dangerous African Americans can be in high places. Ward Connelly and Justice Clarence Thomas are dangerous. They do not act in the best interest of African American people. Walter Williams described earlier the plight of middle-class Black leadership in Washington D.C.

Earlier we looked at the research conducted by the Education Trust on teacher quality and how unfortunate it is that low-income children in schools that are poorly funded and highly segregated are given teachers who are incompetent and not adequately trained to teach particular subjects.

Ruby Payne wants to discuss the significance of family income when the real crime is that our children are being educated by ill prepared teachers. In this chapter we will focus on solutions. So how do we correct this problem?

One option would be to give principals authority to hire and fire the teachers in their schools. It is unfair to hold principals accountable for student outcomes but not give them the ability to hire and fire staff. I don't know one sports coach or one CEO in the business world who would accept that paradigm.

Educational Solutions

As a result of the Teacher Quality study, the state of Wisconsin will make grants available to create mentoring and staff development programs. The state of Michigan passed legislation that forgives 10 percent of state loans for teachers who will work in low-income schools. North Carolina has passed legislation to pay teachers an additional $15,000 to teach math in low-income schools. Hawaii has passed legislation to rehire retired teachers for difficult to fill classroom posts while allowing them to keep their full retirement benefits. Some school districts have provided incentives for their master teachers to teach in challenging areas. Other school districts have offered teachers who teach in challenging areas greater time for development and a smaller teaching load. These are just some of the incentives that are being used to attract and retain talented teachers.

Ideally, unions, superintendents, and parents should prevent teachers who are not certified and did not major in the subject they are attempting to teach from instructing students.

High Achieving Schools

Now let us set our sights on improving schools. There are schools that have been successful at educating low-income students. I want to look at the work of Ron Edmonds and the effective schools model.

The brilliant late superintendent from New York, Ron Edmonds, identified five major factors for effective schools.

1. The principal is the instructional leader.
2. Teachers have high expectations.
3. Students spend more time on task.
4. There is a positive school climate.
5. Testing is used to guide further instruction and not solely for evaluation.

Notice that in his five components of high achieving schools, family income, school funding, and integration are not included. The most important component of an effective school is the principal. I have had the privilege of working with some of the best principals in America.

The least effective principals, probably the ones who believe in the poverty theories, spend the majority of their day in their office. They see themselves as the CEO of the building. They want to manage the budget and the building facility, not faculty, staff, and students.

Ron Edmonds said that the most effective principals are in their offices before the school day begins and after the school day ends, but during the school day, they are visiting classrooms and they are monitoring and helping teachers. They are fully aware of their role as instructional leader of the school. Mt. Vernon, New York, increased test scores from 12 to 90 percent when the superintendent freed principals from cafeteria, bus, playground, and other mundane duties.

Effective principals understand that they have five types of educators in their classrooms. Strong principals make it difficult for custodians, referral agents, and instructors to remain. Strong principals don't just visit a classroom once a year for evaluation. They are there to help their teachers, and the teachers appreciate their expertise.

Strong principals understand that the problem may not be a teacher shortage but a teacher turnover. Forty percent of teachers turn over within five years. In low-achieving schools, you may have a master teacher in Room 201, a new, ineffective teacher in Room 202, and a substitute teacher in Room 203. Is this fair to all the students?

In high-achieving schools, the effective principal will partner new teachers with master teachers, even if this means the principal must cover one of the classrooms. Furthermore, how can a principal be the instructional leader of the school if he or she has not taught a class in the past 20 years?

Effective principals understand the significance of staff development on student outcomes. They provide myriad opportunities for staff in-service training. It is unfortunate that in many low-achieving schools in low-income areas, staff have three days or less of in-service training. One of the ways to measure whether or not a school is serious about educating children is to assess how many hours or days are allocated for in-service training. I have observed districts that waited until the last four days of the school year to provide in-service training. It should be obvious that it was not valued.

The third component of the effective schools model is time on task. More will be said later about this factor when we discuss the KIPP schools, but suffice to say here that effective principals are excellent managers of the school day. In a typical 9:00 to 3:00 day, minus an hour for lunch and recess, theoretically children should receive five hours of instruction. But many teachers and schools lose valuable minutes. If a teacher loses 15 minutes a day, this is not insignificant. Multiply 15 minutes by 5 days a week and the result is 75 minutes. Multiply 75 minutes by a school year, 36 weeks, and the result is two weeks of instruction that have been lost.

Ruby Payne, we could close the achievement gap with workshops on time management. Instead of talking about the bad parents and how poor the children are, teachers should be learning how to make the most of their time with students. Teachers that would rather blame the victims are often guilty of reading their newspapers in class, cutting out food coupons in class, answering their cell phones in class, surfing on their laptops in class, and responding to e-mails in class. They spend more time disciplining than educating children.

Every teacher should learn and apply Rule 555. Ninety-five percent of disciplinary problems come from 5 percent of the students. Most problems occur in the first five and last five minutes of the class period. Master teachers are at their best the first five and last five minutes of the class period. Effective teachers are aware that 5 percent of their students are causing 95 percent of the problems.

The fourth component of the effective schools model is a positive school climate. I can distinguish a low- from a high-achieving school in the first five minutes of my visit. In high-achieving schools, there is a spirit that permeates the entire building that, regardless of family income, school funding, and degree of integration, faculty and staff can make a difference. They have a winning attitude.

In low-achieving schools, teachers make derogatory comments about students in front of their peers, and seldom are they reprimanded. Actually, I believe that those who make derogatory comments are less dangerous than those who stand by and remain silent. They are the ones that reinforce those comments by saying nothing. During slavery, only 10 percent of Whites were slave owners. The other 90 percent, except for a small minority of abolitionists, allowed slavery to flourish.

In high-achieving schools, when you walk through the main corridor, you don't see 46 pictures of White male presidents in a school that is 100 percent Black and Hispanic. In high-achieving schools, students' papers, science exhibits, art, and other works are on full display.

High-achieving schools have created an environment where parents feel welcome. There are activities for parents. Much more will be said about this when we look at the Comer School model and Head Start.

Educational Solutions

The last component of Ron Edmond's effective school model is that testing should be used to guide further instruction and not solely used for evaluation. In high-achieving schools, principals do not allow the school year to be reduced to high-stakes testing. Testing is a reality, but they do not allow tests to burden teachers and students. They also understand that the more relaxed children are when taking tests, the better they will perform. Therefore, rather than taking one high-stakes test at the end of the year, they may be tested monthly, not only to relax the students but also to help teachers assess which areas in the curriculum and pedagogy need adjusting.

The Breakthrough High Schools (BTHS) project involved 25 high schools nationwide in low-income Black and Hispanic neighborhoods. Ninety percent of their students graduated and were accepted into college.

There are approximately 73,000 public schools in America. African American and Hispanic schools are estimated to number 15,000. My major objective as an educational consultant and in this book is to identify high-achieving schools in poor Black and Brown communities. I welcome the research of the Heritage Foundation that identified 21 of those schools. I applaud the Education Trust that identified 1,320 "high flying" schools. The above agencies claim that 15.6 percent of high-poverty schools are high performing.

According to Florida State Professor Doug Harris and Richard Rothstein, author of *Class and Schools,* the two agencies used a questionable methodology. For instance, a school was "high flying" if they were in the highest quartile in only one subject and for only one year. These authors believe it is not 15.6 but rather 1.1 percent.

In response to the critics, the National Center for Educational Accountability (NCEA) researched 20 states and identified 190 schools in poor Black and Brown communities whose students scored in the highest quartile in **multiple** subjects for a minimum of **three** years.[30]

I thank the NCEA for responding to the critics, but I only need one school in a poor Black or Brown community to highlight to all educators that quality education in such schools is not only possible, but it has been achieved. I also remain concerned about critics who want to emphasize economic inequities without economic solutions.

Knowledge Is Power Program

One of the programs I am most proud of and have the utmost respect for is the Knowledge Is Power Program (KIPP). The program was founded in 1994 in Houston, Texas, by two young White males who went beyond Ruby Payne's theory of family income, Kozol's theory of school funding, and Kozol, Orfield, and Holzman's theory of integration. They believe that whatever you do most is what you do best. This relates directly to time on task.

In American schools, not only do we offer fewer school days (180) than Germany (200) and Japan (220) but we poorly manage those 180 days. As I mentioned, in the typical 9:00 to 3:00 school day, 15 minutes per day or two weeks per year is lost. In addition, schools are closed three months during the summer because we still think we are an agrarian economy. Research shows that 80 percent of what children learn during the school year will be lost if not properly reinforced. Therefore, many schools spend the first one to three months of the new school year reviewing what was taught during the last quarter of the previous school year.

There is excellent research reported in *American Sociological Review* and *Phi Delta Kappan* that indicates that a large portion of the racial achievement gap is actually a "summer" phenomenon. Eighty percent of what students learn during the school year is lost during the summer if not properly reinforced. We could close the racial academic achievement gap with either mandatory summer academic programs or divide the 12 week summer vacation into 4 equal breaks of three weeks spread evenly throughout the school year. KIPP understands this and offers 6 additional weeks in the summer. Schools are doing a better job than they have been given credit for. It is when school is not in session that poor children suffer. If schools do not want to do this, they should compare test scores between fall and spring which would exclude summer. Unfortunately, many schools compare test scores between spring and spring, this includes summer which is detrimental for many low-income youth. Why are we closing schools during the summer? We are no longer living in an agrarian economy.[31]

In the KIPP model, school stays open year round. Children go on vacation 6 weeks during the summer rather than 12 weeks. I know of schools that are on a rotating schedule of 9 weeks of instruction and 3 weeks of vacation—and that's repeated 4 times throughout the year.

The KIPP school day runs from approximately 8:00 am to 5:00 pm, Monday through Friday, 9:00 am to 1:00 pm every other Saturday, and adds six additional weeks during the summer. The major component at KIPP is simply greater time on task. It is not that they have bought into the Ron Edmonds effective schools model, although many KIPP schools have. It is not that they have bought into more right-brain lesson plans, although many KIPP schools understand that Black and Hispanic children are often oral learners. It is not that they have made their curriculum more Africentric, although some have. The major component of KIPP is simply an expanded school calendar. Teachers, parents, and students sign a contract, agreeing to give their best effort.

Let me share some of the results of the KIPP program. Since its inception, 80 percent of KIPP students have earned acceptance to college compared to only 48 percent of public high seniors in New York and Houston. KIPP students have earned more than $13 million in scholarships to four-year universities. One hundred percent of eighth graders of the first three KIPP schools to open now attend public, private, and parochial high schools throughout the United States. The average first-year KIPP student enters 5th grade at the 28th percentile but progresses to the 74th percentile by 8th grade graduation. Ninety percent of the students are Black and Hispanic and 80 percent receive free lunch.

KIPP eighth grade students have earned more than $21 million in high school scholarships. The KIPP school in Washington, DC, the Key Academy, is the highest performing public middle school in the District of Columbia. KIPP Gaston College Preparatory in Gaston, North Carolina, is a North Carolina school of excellence. One hundred percent of last year's eighth graders achieved above-grade-level scores. At KIPP Hartwood Academy in San Jose, California, the fifth grade outperformed every other fifth grade in the school district. They were the highest performing fifth grade in math among all California charter schools.

KIPP's South Fulton Academy, East Point, Georgia, sixth grade had the highest passing rate in math in South Fulton County. KIPP's Summit Academy, San Lorenzo, California, sixth grade outperformed every single school in the district in every subject on the California Standards Test. KIPP's Ujima Village Academy, Baltimore, Maryland, fifth grade, earned the highest fifth grade math scores in Baltimore. KIPP Ways Academy, Atlanta, Georgia, was one of the ten schools in Atlanta with a 100 percent passing rate on the state's fifth-grade writing test.

Educational Solutions

I've had the privilege of providing numerous workshops for KIPP. In my training sessions to non-KIPP teachers, I often show the KIPP tape so that frustrated teachers can see with their own eyes how KIPP schools in low-income areas produce Black and Hispanic students well above the national average.

Ruby Payne, it is not family income. It is time on task. Whatever you do most will be what you do best.

Single Gender

The next solution comes from the National Association of Single Sex Public Education. This is a clearinghouse of single-gender classrooms and schools. They did not create the concept.

In the late 1980s and early 1990s, I worked with principals in Detroit (Malcolm X Academy, Marcus Garvey, and Paul Robeson) to advocate for single-gender classrooms and schools. The major obstacle was the assumption that single-gender classrooms and schools violated Title 9 legislation regarding gender balance. I never will forget the tremendous challenges that the Malcolm X, Marcus Garvey, and Paul Robeson schools faced in their fight against the ACLU and NOW.

Advocacy of single-gender classrooms and schools was an African-centered response. What does the ACLU and NOW have to do with African American males fighting for survival? Unfortunately, the judge ruled in favor of the ACLU and did not allow the three schools to maintain their single-gender status. Fortunately, the Detroit Black community did not allow the ACLU and NOW to nullify their objections to the ruling. They discouraged African American parents from sending their girls to those schools.

Over the past two decades, NOW and the feminists have grown increasingly frustrated. Although White girls outperform White males academically K-12, this has not been reflected in the professional ranks, especially in math and scientific fields. They have now become supporters of single-gender classrooms in schools. Research says that when females are taught in a single-gender environment and, as Thomas Dee documented, by a female teacher, they become more confident in math and science. They pursue careers in engineering, accounting, computer programming, and medicine.

Over the past decade, the courts have been more willing to accept single-gender classrooms in schools as long as the district will provide the same resources equally for both genders. As a result, if you visit the website of the National Association for Single Sex Public Education (NASSPE), you will find more than 500 classrooms and 100 schools. It is much easier to implement the single-gender classroom than single-gender school, and many principals have been willing to do that at a far greater rate than superintendents. I encourage principals to be committed to the program and not try it for just one period or one year.

I have been advocating for single-gender schools since 1985. Let me give two examples of success with such schools.

The first is the Thurgood Marshall Elementary School in Seattle, Washington. Before they implemented single-gender classrooms, the male students were in the 16 percentile on the state achievement exam. After they implemented single-gender, those same boys tested at the 72 percentile.

The Women's Leadership Academy in Harlem graduated over 90 percent of their girls, and more than 90 percent were admitted into college. Teen pregnancy is at an all time low. Single-gender classrooms also reduce suspensions, special education placements, and the dropout rate.

Educational Solutions

The last time I looked, Ruby Payne, the boys in Seattle and the girls in Harlem were low income, and few of their mothers possessed a college degree. Yet in spite of family income, school funding, and segregation, single-gender classrooms and schools have produced students well above the national average.

Africentricity

The next solution is the concept of African-centered schools and multicultural curriculums. I have never met a child who associated being smart with being White who knew that Imhotep, not Hippocrates, was the first doctor, or that the father of mathematics was not Pythagoras, but Ahmose. I have never met a Black child who associated being smart with being White and knew that his ancestors built the pyramids.

Before we look at public African-centered schools and charter schools, I must give credit where credit is due, to the Council of Independent Black Institutions (CIBI). These private schools, which came into existence in 1972, do not agree with Ruby Payne's poverty theory. They believe that when you teach African American children their history and culture, academic performance and self-esteem will improve. These schools see few fights and suspensions because the children are grounded in their history and culture. They are taught the Nguzo Saba and Maat.

These schools understand that you do not address disciplinary problems and violence with a metal detector. That's a band-aid. If you want to get to the root of the problem, you must teach children values. My career began in a CIBI school in Chicago. In its heyday, there were more than 100 CIBI schools, ranging from preschool through high school. CIBI students, historically, have tested well above the national average.

The major problem that CIBI schools have always faced is financing. Because CIBI schools are private schools designed to educate African American children regardless of income, they have to charge tuition. Consequently, the very people they want to serve are often unable to afford it. Historically, CIBI has done everything possible to provide scholarships, but the reality is that someone has to pay. While many private schools charge $400 to $1,000 per month, CIBI schools have tried to keep tuition between $100 and $300 per month. With tuition that low, it is difficult to hire and maintain staff.

Ironically, as much as I'm in favor of teacher quality and the need for teachers to be qualified in their subject areas, the amazing thing about CIBI schools is that many teachers lack a college degree or did not major in the subject they teach. However, they are able to compensate for that with a tremendous love for students and an Africentric curriculum.

There has been a splintering of CIBI schools. Many of the directors who administered those schools over the past 20 years, a tremendous labor of love, have grown weary and broke. One of the ways they have been able to overcome this is by becoming African-centered charter schools. They now are on the public school payroll, but they have been able to maintain, all things considered, the integrity of the Africentric curriculum model.

Let me describe just a couple of those schools. In Kansas City, in 1996, Ladd became an African-centered school. In 1998, less than 10 percent of the third graders scored at the highest level in reading on the statewide assessment. In 2002, 72 percent were at the highest level. Ninety-two percent of those students qualified for free or reduced-price lunch. It has become one of the best schools in the state of Missouri.

Another school in Kansas City is Chick. On the Missouri assessment program fourth grade math test, 48 percent of Chick students tested at the proficient or advanced level. Statewide only 24 percent of Black students and 36 percent of White students scored that high.

Another example is the Woodlawn School in Chicago. All the students are Black. Nearly 74 percent of third graders met or exceeded state standards in reading. Eighty-three percent achieved the same level in math. More than half the students at Woodlawn are either below the poverty line or low-income.

Ruby Payne, we can negate the poverty theory with an Africentric curriculum. I have been pleased that many of these schools have used our SETCLAE K-12 curriculum (Self-Esteem Through Culture Leads to Academic Excellence) and our *Lessons from History* textbook.

HBCUs

The next solution comes from historically Black colleges and universities (HBCUs). Even though this book is concerned with students K-12, we can learn from the HBCU model. It has a lot to teach those who think that family income, school funding, and integration are the most important factors in student achievement.

How do we explain that HBCUs only have 16 percent of African American college students but produce 30 percent of the graduates? How do we explain Howard's greater success at graduating African American students than Harvard—yet, Kozol, Harvard has more money. If you're suffering from a little racism, you may think it's easier to graduate from Howard than Harvard. If you believe that, then how do you explain that 75 percent of African Americans who earn a graduate degree from a White university were undergraduates at a Black college? If Black colleges are inferior, how could their graduates go on to a White universities and earn graduate degrees?

What are Black colleges doing that K-12 schools could imitate? How do we explain that the school that had the greatest placement of students in medical school is not Harvard, Yale, or Princeton, but Xavier? Xavier has a 92 percent placement of their pre-med students in medical schools. What can we learn from Xavier and their science department? What can we learn from Howard in the teaching of law and communications? What can we learn from Florida A&M in the area of business instruction? What can we learn from North Carolina A&T in teaching engineering? What can we learn from Hampton, Tuskegee, Spelman, and Morehouse about instilling leadership qualities?

Why is it that so many African Americans who barely graduate from White universities have no desire to pursue graduate school? Because their spirits have been broken. Yet HBCU graduates enthusiastically and confidently pursue graduate degrees from White universities. Could Thomas Dee be correct that the racial makeup of the faculty is extremely important? It is possible for an African American college student to go to a White university and never take a class from an African American professor. HBCU students, however, can proudly say they have learned from African American professors.

HBCUs are successful because they realize that self-esteem is still important. Seldom will you hear on a Black college campus that acting smart is acting White. Kozol, that conflict came out of integration. Why do so many Black colleges

138

have weekly or monthly convocations? Why do they feel a need on a weekly or monthly basis to bring in a motivational speaker to inspire the students? If self-esteem is important at the adult level, then surely educators K-12 must realize the importance of esteem-building assembly programs on a weekly or monthly basis.

Comer Schools

I encourage you to read James Comer, Jr.'s books, but especially *Leave No Child Behind* and *Maggie's American Dream.* There are hundreds of Comer schools nationwide that do not subscribe to Ruby Payne's poverty theory. However, they do believe in collaboration among schools, parents, and the community.

The Comer school model is based on a team approach, and three teams make the model work.

The school planning and management team develops a comprehensive school plan that sets academic, social, and community relations goals and coordinates all school activities, including staff development programs. The team creates critical dialogue concerning teaching and learning and monitors progress to identify needed adjustments to the school plan as well as opportunities to support the plan. Members of the team include administrators, teachers, support staff, and parents.

The student and staff support team promotes desirable social conditions and relationships. It connects all of the school's students and student services, facilitates the sharing of information and advice, addresses individual student needs, accesses resources outside the school, and develops prevention programs. Serving on this team are the principal and staff members with expertise in child development and mental health, such as counselors, social workers, psychologists, and nurses.

The parent team involves parents in the school by developing activities through which the parent can support the school's social and academic programs. This team also selects representatives to serve on the school planning and management team.

Comer schools have reduced absenteeism and suspensions and have improved test scores. Comer schools are in low-income areas. They are poorly funded and highly segregated. What I respect most about the Comer schools is that rather than blaming parents, they make them a part of the team and empower them.

The same is true for Head Start. Ruby Payne. Read the biography of Maxine Waters, the brilliant congresswoman from California whose origin was in Head Start. Head Start saw something valuable in Maxine. They empowered her to become a teacher's assistant, teacher, and director. She then went on to the state senate and then the U.S. Congress.

Ruby Payne and her staff should read the work of Mavis Sanders, which is similar to the work of James Comer. In her book *Building School Community Partnerships,* she describes the following:

Student Centered
Student awards
Student incentives
Scholarships
Student trips
Tutors
Mentors
Job shadowing and other services and products for students

Educational Solutions

Family Centered
Parent workshops
Family fun nights
GED and other adult education classes
Parent incentives and rewards
Counseling and other forms of assistance

Community Centered
Community beautification
Student exhibits and performances
Charity and other outreach

Unfortunately, most schools are school-centered, not student- family- or community-centered. Let me give a picture of an institution that is school-centered. The school determines the day, the time, the topic, and the location of the PTA meeting. I am always disappointed when I am scheduled to speak at a PTA meeting and staff members try to convince me that only 10 or 20 parents are expected to attend because of apathy, income, and educational background. If that's what they think, that's what they're going to receive.

Why is the meeting scheduled at 9:00 am, 12:00 noon, or 3:00 pm rather than in the evening? Is it because the teachers who do not live in the neighborhood are afraid to return for an evening workshop? Has the meeting been scheduled for staff rather than parents? Can you imagine Wal-Mart telling their customers that they're only going to be open Monday, Wednesday, and Friday from 9:00 to 12:00?

Why are the Individualized Educational Plan (IEP) meetings that determine special ed placement designed for staff and not parents? Why do parents have to miss work for a PTA meeting, graduation, or IEP meeting? Why are the meetings always at the school and not the church or community center?

141

Family-centered schools realize that many parents would feel more comfortable attending the meeting at the church or community center rather than in the school. If schools are sincere about increasing parental involvement, they should consider the day, the time, and the location of meetings.

Who determines the topic? If we know that parents are younger these days and less mature, then before giving the workshop on their child's development, maybe we should give them a workshop on their own development. Ruby Payne, if you're so concerned about economics and poverty, if you want the fathers to be there, you may need to offer workshops on employment, economic development, and entrepreneurship.

Parents know when they're welcome and when they're not. There are schools in the inner city that were built 100 years ago, seemingly with the same secretary still cutting parents off at the door. Maybe that's why in Comer and Head Start schools there are parent coordinators, a parents room, and parents are made to feel welcome.

As Gary MacDougal documented, the schools that have been effective in increasing parental involvement provide childcare and transportation. The schools that have really become successful at attracting parents understand the importance of providing food. I don't mean refreshments; I mean a meal.

Head Start

Head Start has documented their success over the years, but only 40 percent of eligible children are able to attend. On the other hand, middle-income and affluent parents are often willing to spend up to $22,000 to enroll their children in "Baby Ivies" or day care. The government can find money for Iraq and for prisons but not for cost-effective programs such as Head Start, Title 1, and Pell Grants.

Educational Solutions

In addition to educating students and empowering parents, Head Start provides medical support for children. More than 50 percent of low-income children have visual problems. If the visual problems were corrected by providing eyeglasses and eye exercises, we could improve academic achievement. Last year, Head Start provided more than 800,000 poor children with medical and dental screenings and immunizations. Sixty-five thousand received mental health assessments, and 75,000 received assistance with speech or language impairment.

Chicago Child Parent Centers participated in a long-term study of more than 550 children. The six-year study started at age 2 and continued through age 8. The students scored higher in reading through seventh grade and had lower rates of grade retention and special education placement than comparable children who had not received preschool intervention. There are over 800,000 low-income preschoolers who do not attend preschool programs. It is estimated that these programs could close the achievement gap by over 25 percent.[32]

Vision Care

At the Mather School in Boston, a team of optometrists conducted a six-year demonstration, identifying and treating vision problems of low-income children, the sort of problems that typically go uncorrected in low-income schools. The optometrists collected test scores and grades as well and reported that children who received glasses gained 4.5 percentile points per year on reading tests compared to children without vision problems, who gained 0.6 percentile points a year.

We spend so much time looking at family income, the educational background of the mother, the school's per pupil expenditure, and the racial makeup of the school while the reality is that if we simply provided children with an eye exam, eye therapy, and glasses, we could improve academic performance.

Bill Gates Foundation

Bill Gates believes that smaller school size is the key to academic success. The Gates are applying what they have learned to New York City, their most ambitious effort to transform a school district. Their foundation has pumped in more than $100 million since 2000 to help create some 150 new small schools that currently enroll more than 50,000 students. Most are only partly full since they typically start with the ninth grade and add a new grade each year.

Some of the campaign's most hopeful early returns have come from New York in part because the foundation has worked effectively with New Visions for Public Schools, a local nonprofit with long experience developing small schools. In 2006, the first 14 of 78 new small high schools that Gates created with New Visions will hold their first graduations. About 70 percent of the students who began ninth grade four years ago are expected to graduate. That's double the rate of the larger schools they replaced and well above the city's 54 percent graduation rate.

If it can happen in the South Bronx, it can happen just about anywhere. What was one of the worst schools in the city, South Bronx High, is now home to Mott Haven Village Preparatory High School, a 325-student enclave on one and one-half floors of the old school building. In June 2006, at least 80 percent of the students that started four years ago will graduate. Of those, 70 percent have been accepted by a college. The graduation rate at the old South Bronx High School was less than 50 percent. Although only about half of all New

Educational Solutions

York high school students passed the state's regent's exam needed to graduate, 96 percent of Mott Haven students passed. Florida and Mississippi have decided to reduce the dropout rate and student boredom by allowing high school students to select a major. Therefore, out of 24 classes, they can select four classes in their major.

Metwest High School in Oakland, California, is a rebel in the world of public education. It thrives on breaking the rules and succeeding. Today, all 25 seniors, among them a girl in foster care, an undocumented immigrant, and several students from families where high school diplomas are rare and college degrees nonexistent, will walk the stage with a diploma in one hand and college acceptance in the other. Every senior in the unorthodox school's graduating class has been accepted to a four-year college, a rare achievement for many urban public schools.

The school of 130 students operates under the philosophy of educational reformers Dennis Littky and Elliot Washor, cofounders of The Big Picture, an organization that has opened 40 schools across the country in the last 10 years. The method personalizes student education based on their strengths and interests. Real world experiences are stressed as important learning tools in direct instruction and testing. At Metwest there are no final exams, no letter grades, and no bells herding students through crowded hallways. Students spend only three days a week in the classroom. The other two days they serve as interns at hospitals, government agencies, schools, and community organizations.

In most high schools, students go to different classes, turn in their work, and go home. At Metwest, students have to think critically about what they are doing. They have personalized schedules and move freely among their internships. Academic classes and courses are taken at Laney College. Instead of final exams, students typically prepare projects, organize a health fair for Spanish-speaking immigrants, or establish a school debate team under the guidance of a mentor at their internship site.

They are doing things that matter and have value outside the classroom. It's the difference between doing an English paper on a dead poet or a brochure for an animal hospital that will improve the well-being of pets. Independence and responsibility are being developed.

Metwest requires seniors to apply to at least six colleges. This year, graduates sent out 175 applications and received $270,000 in scholarships. This is the kind of creativity that we need if we're going to be effective.

The success at Metwest reinforces my position that we can reduce the dropout rate if we make the curriculum relevant. I recommend the following street curriculum:

Map out a neighborhood with a 10-block radius.
Teach geography using the neighborhood.
How many liquor stores?
How many fast food stores? Supermarkets?
How many barber, beauty, and nail salons?
Describe gang turf.
Where are the drug houses?
What do people ages 18-30 do between 7 am-7 pm?
What is the unemployment level?
What is the extent of STDs and AIDS?
What is the teen pregnancy level?
Where are the boarded and vacant buildings?
What are the recreation options during the weekday and weekend?
What are the top five crimes?
What is the extent of fatherlessness?

Educational Solutions

How clean is the neighborhood?
Who are the police officers?
What is the 100-year history of the neighborhood?
If you were the mayor, what would you do to improve the neighborhood?
Where are the billboards and what do they promote?
Where are the churches and what are they doing?
What do you like best in the neighborhood?
How many stores are owned by African Americans, Arabs, Asians, Whites, and Hispanics? What is the largest African American business?
Where can a child buy cigarettes and liquor?

The teacher should use the above exercises and integrate them into reading, writing, math, history, geography, and science curriculums.

I am a strong advocate of smaller schools. Schools are not factories, and we should not design a school system that mirrors a factory approach to education. Enrolling 2,000 to 5,000 students with three to five counselors is deplorable and unacceptable.

Ruby Payne, one of the best ways to address poverty is to imitate Warren Buffett. He put his money on the table, $37 billion to the Gates Foundation, because he knew and respected what Gates could do with the money.

Departmentalization

I am not in favor of departmentalization. My research and that of others have documented the decline of African American students' test scores from the fourth grade on. One major reason for this is departmentalization. With each passing grade, the number of teachers a child sees is increased. I agree with Ruby Payne about the importance of the relationship

147

between teacher and student. In large high schools and some elementary schools where students have four to seven teachers per day, students can get lost.

Even at the high school level, departmentalization can be reduced. While at the elementary school level it may be possible for the fourth, sixth, or eighth grade teacher to teach all subjects, that may not be possible at the high school level. Rather than installing a different teacher for algebra, geometry, trig, and calculus, I would employ only one math teacher, and he/she would teach all four of those subjects. The same applies to science; I would only have one science teacher to teach biology, chemistry, and physics. I would ensure that students had the same English teacher, history teacher, and physical education teacher for all four years.

Small Classrooms

Another success model that we need to learn from is showcased in the research of the Students/Teachers Achievement Ratio (STAR). It provides the most definitive findings yet on the effects of reducing class size vis-à-vis student achievement. In 1985 the STAR project started a longitudinal study in Tennessee that followed kindergarten through third-grade students who were placed in small classes of between 13 and 17 students. The control group attended regular-size classes. The study monitored both groups' reading and math achievement each year. Students who had been assigned to the smaller classes scored significantly higher on reading and math tests.

A follow-up study found that when the STAR students reached eighth grade, those who had been in smaller classes until third grade continued to outperform the control group. Minority students achieved the greatest gains. A later follow-up study of STAR students found that by high-school graduation, children originally in smaller classes showed superior educational outcomes than peers in larger classes. Throughout their school careers, STAR students continued to show higher levels of achievement, better grade point averages, and higher rates of on-time graduation. The students in smaller classes were also more likely to graduate in the top 25 percent of the class, less likely to drop out, and more likely to attend college.

The effect of class-size reduction was also studied in Milwaukee's Student Achieving and Guarantee in Education program (SAGE). They reported gains similar to those of STAR. SAGE reported that the largest academic gains for African American males were in smaller classes. Another similar study of 200 school districts found smaller class size raised math achievement by six months, with low-income students living in urban areas making the largest gains.[33]

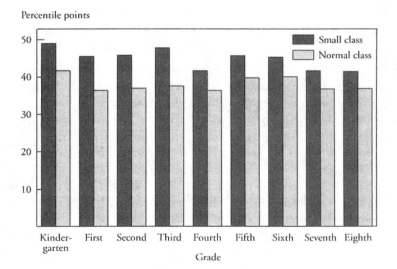

With every grade, the research showed an increase in academic achievement, regardless of family income, educational background of the family, school funding, or the racial makeup of the school. There is a 5 to 10 percent gap when comparing smaller classes to regular class sizes. Ruby Payne, the issue is not poverty, but class size.

Homework

I agree with Ruby Payne regarding homework. Some teachers expect parents to become their assistant teachers in the area of homework. This is a middle-class approach. They expect parents to teach children concepts that were not thoroughly covered in class. Some teachers even assume that every home has a chemistry set, a microscope, and Internet access.

Ruby Payne cited a successful middle school in Texas that schedules the last 45 minutes of every day for homework support. I agree with this approach. Students who did not get their homework done must go to the cafeteria where tutors are available to help with assignments. More and more schools need to develop homework labs. The founders of the KIPP Academy asked the principal if they could stay after school for one hour because they noticed that students were not doing their homework or studying for quizzes and tests. These two instructors stayed one additional hour for the remainder of the school year with their students and saw a tremendous increase in test scores.

I also agree with author Alfie Kohn who wrote *The Homework Myth*. He documents that there are no definitive studies documenting the significance of homework. I believe in time on task, and my desire is to increase African American study time and reduce time watching television, playing video games, and listening to gangsta rap, I am not in favor of meaningless, boring homework which could contribute to our dropout rate. **Quantity does not mean quality. Homework should be meaningful.** Children do not need 100 additional problems if they mastered 10 in class. If they did not, doing 100 at home without a teacher is futile. Unfortunately, many schools expect parents to achieve at home what they could not teach in class. I am in favor of reading for pleasure during homework or when children are learning via discovery. Earlier, I mentioned our street curriculum. I strongly advocate that homework involve community empowerment.

The Efficacy Program

The Efficacy Program was created by Jeff Howard in Boston. The program is based on the concept that we need to teach students how to win. One of the major components of Efficacy is the "psychology of performance." This reinforces the approach of HBCUs and convocations. We need to teach children how to win. When children are taught the psychology of performance, they no longer associate being smart with being White.

There are four attributes to the psychology of performance: ability, effort, luck, and the nature of the task.

A student with high self-esteem and confidence would attribute receiving a grade of 100 on an exam to either to ability or effort. That's how winners think. If the same student received a 40 on the exam, he would never question his ability. He would simply study harder. These students understand the KIPP model, whatever you do most is what you do best. Therefore, this student would not drop the class or question his ability. He would try harder. He would increase his study hours. That's how winners think.

Unfortunately, a student with low self-esteem who receives 100 on the test would attribute the grade to either luck or the nature of the test. If he received a 40 on the test, he would question his ability, which means he would not try harder.

I get concerned when 200 African American males try out for the basketball team at an integrated school, knowing that 188 of them will not make the team. Few if any try for the debate team and science fair team. The beauty in life is in the attempt, and when they do not try, it shows and confirms what they think of themselves.

Every school should implement the Efficacy Program and teach their children the psychology of performance. This was reinforced in a longitudinal study of 140 eighth grade students. Self-discipline measured by a self report, parent report, teacher report, and monetary choice questionnaires in the fall predicted final grades, school attendance, standardized achievement test results, and selection into a competitive high school program the following spring.

In a replication with another 164 eighth graders, a behavioral delay of gratification task, a questionnaire on student study habits, and a group-administered IQ test were added. Self-discipline measured in the fall counted for more than twice as much variance as IQ and final grades. High school selection, school attendance, hours spent doing homework, hours spent watching television, and the time of day students began their homework also counted. The effect of self-discipline on final grades held even when controlling for first marking period grades, achievement test scores, and measured IQ.

These findings suggest that the reason why students fall short of their intellectual potential is their failure to exercise self-discipline.

Educational Solutions

Test Taking Courses

Ruby Payne, is the disparity in test scores due to the fact that middle-income families and above actually pay for better scores? The Princeton Review guarantees a 3-point increase on the ACT and a 200-point increase on the SAT. Should we study poverty or simply provide all children with free test-taking classes? Students score higher the more times they take the exam. More affluent students take the PSAT as early as 5th grade. Unfortunately, many poor students take the SAT in the last semester of their senior year. We could close the gap if we provided the opportunity for low-income students to test earlier.

The Challenge

I want to challenge parents, the larger community, and churches. I want to recommend Bishop Williamson's concept of "one church, one school." There are 85,000 churches in Black America and less than 15,000 schools with African American students. Every church should adopt a school.

A principal in Forth Worth, Texas was having academic challenges in her school and called upon local churches. They responded and test scores moved from last to third among 20 schools. In Baltimore, a principal was having security problems and called Bethel AME to provide assistance. They responded and children now feel safe and ready to learn. I challenge every church to adopt a high school freshman male class and mentor them until graduation. The Black male dropout rate in most cities hovers near 50 percent. This is unacceptable. In addition, every church and community organization needs to offer a Saturday Academy. This program will include tutorial, test taking skills, African history, mentoring, and rites of passage. This has been very successful for the Asian and

Jewish community. If we did this, it would not only improve academics, but reduce if not eliminate the use of the "N" word. More importantly, every school should work with the community to develop a Saturday academy. The success of Asian and Jewish communities is due to Saturday academies. My company, African American Images, has a Saturday academy. The W.E.B. DuBois Learning Center in Kansas City is another excellent Saturday academy.

Saturday academies tutor children, help them with test-taking skills, and teach them their history and culture. Jewish and Asian children are not smarter than African American and Hispanic children. They are the beneficiaries of Saturday academies. In the spirit of the Comer model, I challenge every school to create partnerships with the larger community so that every school has a Saturday academy.

American schools should look at Cuba, with their literacy rate of greater than 90 percent. In America, literacy is 70 percent and even less in Black and Hispanic communities. There are many reasons why Cuba is more successful than America, but it is not because their families have more income. It is not because their mothers are better educated. It is not because their schools are better funded. It is because of their will. They put the emphasis on the collective and not the individual. There is less class distinction in Cuba than in America.

American schools still believe in tracking. American schools reflect capitalism. The naive premise from which I've been operating throughout this book and in all of my work is that schools should educate all children. If that is so, then American schools have failed. That's why I'm so adamant about what must be done to educate all children.

Educational Solutions

But it may be that schools are very successful because schools are designed to reinforce capitalism, classism, educate the haves, and miseducate the have-nots. The game is called tracking. We say that education is for the children. If that were so, we would abolish tracking. All the research from Jeanie Oakes and numerous others documents the fact that tracking is beneficial to teachers and terrible for children.

The Rockville School District in New York decided they were going to close the achievement gap by closing the curriculum gap. They dismantled tracking. Before tracking only 23 percent of African Americans and Hispanics passed the first Regent's math exam. After abolishing tracking, the figure rose to 75 percent.[35] If schools are unwilling to abolish tracking, they should open AP, honors, and gifted and talented classes to all students with no prerequisites. African American students should be encouraged if not mandated to attend. Ruby Payne, poverty persists, but the gap closed when they abolished tracking.

For all those who believe Charles Murray and *The Bell Curve,* if the problem was genetic, the achievement gap between Black and White students would be just as large in kindergarten as it is in twelfth grade. It is not. The gap widens with each passing grade. One reason for this is tracking.

AP, honors, and gifted and talented students enjoy a smaller student-teacher ratio, better teachers, and a curriculum that is challenging. Teachers ask open-ended questions, and students are encouraged to ask questions. This is far different from the regular, remedial, and special ed classes that Martin Haberman talks about in *The Pedagogy of Poverty,* where students are not encouraged to ask questions, and teachers ask questions with predetermined answers. Teachers in lower-skill classes are not as c capable as those in the advanced classes. If America were serious about closing the achievement gap and eliminating classism, should not the students in regular, remedial, and special ed receive the best teachers, smaller student-teacher ratios, and an advanced curriculum and pedagogy?

If we are serious about closing the racial academic achievement gap and empowering low-income children, then we must give them school choices between the public and private sector. Monopolies are not effective. They are no more effective in schools than they are in industry. Let me provide an example.

I'm a frequent flyer. I noticed that the two major airlines flying from Chicago to Baltimore were charging $600 round trip. When Southwest Airlines entered the market, for some strange reason American and United learned how to fly from Chicago to Baltimore for $200. Do you think American and United would have reduced their prices without the entry of Southwest Airlines? The answer is no.

Ruby Payne, until low-income children are given a choice, the same privilege that middle-class parents have, then this problem may continue to persist unless schools become serious about implementing all the other suggestions that I have recommended.

Milwaukee is an example of a city that has implemented a school choice program that broke the public school monopoly. Families who sent their students to voucher schools had a graduation rate of 64 percent, compared to only 36 percent of African American males who attended Milwaukee public schools.

If we are serious about education, we can no longer allow educational unions, business vendors, special interests, and poverty theorists to control our school systems.

Educational Solutions

Any **one** of the above solutions can save low-income children who reside in racially segregated neighborhoods and attend poorly funded schools. Can you imagine if we used them **all**?

I hope you have benefited from this book, and I pray educators will focus on that which we control, namely, expectations, time on task, curriculum, pedagogy, and single-gender classrooms, and leave poverty issues to the economists.

REFERENCES

1. Valencia, Richard. *The Evolution of Deficit Thinking.* Washington: The Falmer Press, 1997, p. 3.

2. ibid., p. 115.

3. Rothstein, Richard. *Class and Schools.* Washington: Economic Policy Institute, 2004, pp. 54-55.

4. The National Center for Fair and Open Testing.

5. Payne, Ruby. *A Framework for Understanding Poverty.* Highlands, Texas: Aha, 2001, p. 79.

6. *Education Week*, November 3, 1999. *Washington Post*, July 6, 2004.

7. Rothstein, op.cit., p. 49.

8. Ogbu, John. *Minority Education and Caste.* New York: Academic Press, 1978, pp. 357, 369.

9. Anderson, Claud. *Black Labor White Wealth.* Edgewood, Maryland: Duncan and Duncan, 1994, pp. 133-134.

10. Hacker, Andrew. *Two Nations.* New York: Charles Scribners, 1992, pp. 31-32.

11. *Black Enterprise Magazine.* June 2006, p. 86.

12. Kunjufu, Jawanza. *Solutions for Black America.* Chicago: African American Images, 2004, p. 120.

13. Kozol, Jonathan. *Savage Inequalities.* New York: Crown, 1991, p. 16.

14. Kozol, Jonathan. *Shame of a Nation.* New York: Crown, 2005, p. 50.

15. Rothstein, op.cit., p. 37.

16. Williams, Walter. "Who Is to Blame?" *Washington Times,* July 7, 2006.

17. Dial, Karla. "LA Parents Sue," *School Reform News,* May, 2006, pp. 1, 16.

18. Holzman, Michael. "The Effects of Segregation on Black Boys," *Education Week,* January 4, 2006, pp. 29-30.

19. *Black Enterprise Magazine*, August 2006, p. 45.

20. Kozol, op.cit., *Shame of a Nation,* p. 8.

21. ibid., p. 19.

22. Cashin, Sheryll. *The Failures of Integration.* New York: Perseus, 2004, pp. 64, 156.

23. Hacker, op.cit., p. 36.

24. Cashin, op.cit., p. 8.

25. "New Study Explores Views of Black and White Parents," www.publicagenda.org.

26. Woodson, Robert. *The Triumphs of Joseph.* New York: Free Press, 1998, p. 19.

27. Jacobson, Linda. "Study: Quality of 1st Grade Teachers Plays Key Role," *Education Week Magazine,* September 21, 2005, pp. 3, 16.

28. Haberman, Martin. "The Pedagogy of Poverty vs. Good Teaching," *Phi Delta Kappan*, December 1991, pp. 290-294.

29. Dee, Thomas. "Teachers, Race and Student Achievement." National Bureau of Economic Research: August 2001, No. W8432.

30. Olson, Lynn. "Sleuths Seek Secrets of High-Flying School," *Education Week,* May 4, 2005.

31. Entwisle, Doris R., and Karl L. Alexander. "Summer Setback: Race, Poverty, School Composition, and Mathematics Achievement in the First Two Years of School," *American Sociological Review*, vol. 57, 1992, pp. 72-84; Richard Allington and Anne McGill-Franzen. "The Impact of Summer Setback on the Reading Achievement Gap," *Phi Delta Kappan*, September 2003, pp. 68-75; and Gerald W. Bracey. "Summer Loss: The Phenomenon No One Wants to Deal With," *Phi Delta Kappan*, September 2002, pp. 12-13.

32. Haskins, Ron, and Cecilia Rouse. "Closing Achievement Gaps," *The Future of Children,* Spring, 2005, pp. 3-5.

33. Kunjufu, Jawanza. *Black Students—Middle-Class Teachers.* Chicago: African American Images, 2002, pp. 147-148.

34. Chubb, John, and Tom Loveless. *Bridging the Achievement Gap.* Washington: Brookings Press, 2002, p. 25.

35. Burris, Carol, and Kevin Welner. "Closing the Achievement Gap by Detracking," *Phi Delta Kappan,* April 2005, pp. 594-597.

INDEX

Asante, Molefi xiii

Call Me Mister 122

Carson, Ben 12

CIBI 135, 136

Comer, James 12, 139, 140

Cuba xi, 85, 154

Dee, Thomas 120, 122-124, 134, 138

Edmonds, Ron 125, 126, 131

Education Trust v, 113, 124, 129

Gates, Bill 4, 52, 144, 147

HBCU 137, 138, 151

Head Start 12, 128, 140, 142, 143

Jackson, Jesse vi

KIPP 127, 130-132, 150, 151

Kozol, Jonathan v, xviii, 3, 72, 92, 94, 96, 97, 100-102, 104,
    115, 119, 122, 123, 130, 137, 138

165

Maafa xiv

Maat 15, 66, 135

MacDougal, Gary 13, 71, 142

Mariotti, Steve 53

Meeks, James v, vi, 78

NAACP 15, 97

Nguzo Saba 66, 135

Ogbu, John xvi, 3, 32, 42

Orfield, Gary 92, 94, 100-102, 115, 119, 122, 123, 130

Reparations 36, 38, 70, 71

Sanders, William 80, 105, 106, 109, 113, 124, 140

Schott Foundation 89, 92, 94, 104

Sizemore, Barbara viii, ix

TESA 81, 116, 124

Waters, Maxine 12, 140

Woodson, Robert xii, 47

SCHOOL SETS

Educators' Library * 22 BOOKS * $199.95

Black History Curriculum (SETCLAE)
67 BOOKS, teachers' manual, and other products * $595.00
(specify grade)

Hispanic History and Culture * 40 BOOKS * $320.00

Biographies * 49 BOOKS (cloth) $1,499.95

Multicultural Videos * (20) * $595.00

Hip Hop Street Curriculum (Motivation - Self-Esteem)
80 BOOKS and teachers' manual $499.95 (specify grade)

Parent Set * 22 BOOKS * $199.95

Male - In-house suspension set * 50 BOOKS * $399.95
(specify grade)

Female - In-house suspension set * 50 BOOKS * $399.95
(specify grade)

Posters Set * (230) * $399.99

Free Shipping

African American Images, Inc.
Phone: (773) 445-0322
Fax: (773) 445-9844
customer@africanamericanimages.com
www.africanamericanimages.com
1909 W. 95th St., Chicago, Illinois 60643

NOTES

NOTES

NOTES

NOTES

NOTES

NOTES

NOTES